(Luke7:41 – 43, KJV):

*41 There was a certain cred... debtors: the one owed five hur... other fifty.*

*42 And when they had nothing to pay, he frankly forgave them both. Tell me therefore, which of them will love him most?*

*43 Simon answered and said, I suppose that he, to whom he forgave most. And he said unto him, Thou hast rightly judged.*

It takes real courage and fortitude for someone to stand up and declare publicly what his wife has said on live television before millions of viewers around the world, or in a stadium with over thirty thousand present. Mabel, my wife, had the opportunity to travel with Archbishop Gilbert Deya, one of the world's greatest Evangelist who hosts a T.V Ministry called "More than Conqueror" in the UK. The CBN declares his ministry as being "The second largest in the U.K."

On July,4th, 2002, Archbishop Deya was officially invited to have an audience with HM Queen Elizabeth II. He has been a guest of King Mswati II of Swaziland and he also had an audience with the former President of Kenya, Daniel Arap Moi.

On several occasions, my wife Mabel has been asked to host meetings at which many high-ranking officials attended. Mabel has been accompanying Bishop Deya on several crusades and has given her testimony on the deliverance and healing miracle of the power of God in her life. As a Registered Nurse she has been interviewed along with other nurses and doctors to give testimony about the healing of the people who were sick and were healed by the grace of God.

I can remember the first time I saw Mabel was before live TV Audiences at the Gilbert Deya Ministry (G.D.M.) where I had an appointment to minister in song. I truly witnessed God's grace and mercy upon her life because of her tremendous faith in Him.

Rev Joshua C. McCallum.

# Foreword

Most certainly, I want to start by thanking The Good Lord for this great privilege of allowing me to pen this book. I want to give God all the glory and honour.

I also want to thank my editors, Rose Farley and Joshua McCallum. Thanks be to God for the life of Archbishop Gilbert Deya, whom God has anointed to preach the good news of Jesus Christ, heal the sick and cast out devils.

My gratitude goes out to my daughter Farai who typed a part of this manuscript. I love you so much Farai! You are the best daughter in the world! Thanks to all the wonderful deliverance ministers who stood by me through thick and thin. I am grateful also to all the pastors who counselled and comforted me during my many crises. Blessings to Gifty who taught me the practical things I needed to know in order to be effective in His ministry. Vivian thanks for being available anytime I needed you. May God Himself answer your prayers for being such an understanding friend? Thanks also to Marina Huss for introducing me to reading material on spiritual warfare. Pastor and Mrs Bakka taught me how to be judicious in dealing with the public and for this I am grateful. Pastor Godwin and mummy Vania thank you for standing with me through thick and thin. Pastsor Barry Cummings we have been together for a long time. God answer all your prayers. A special thank you and love for my husband for making me his partner. Thanks for being my teacher, encourager, best friend and so much more. We will make it this time in the name of Jesus!

Mabel McCallum.

# Acknowledgements

I want to thank God for the life of Archbishop Gilbert Deya, whom God has anointed to preach the good news of Jesus Christ, heal the sick and cast out devils.

Farai you are the best daughter in the world.

I want to thank also the powerful deliverance ministers who stood with me through it all.
The various pastors who counselled and comforted me in times of crisis thank God for my daughter who typed part of the manuscript of this book for me. I love you so much.

Bless Gifty who taught me the practical things I needed to know in order to be effective in ministry.

Vivian, thank you for being there at anytime let God himself answers your prayers for being such an understanding friend.

Marina Huss, a special thank you for forcing me to read on spiritual warfare.

Pastor and Mrs Bakka, thank you for teaching me to leave people alone if I want the anointing,
Thank you pastor Godwin and Vania Kwawu for always standing with me
 Pastor Barry Cummings you have been there since day one

A special thank you and love for my husband for marrying me. Thank you for being my teacher, confidant, best friend, and all. We will make it this time in the name of Jesus!

# Table of Contents

# Introduction

Evil forces used to overwhelm me. I longed to be a free woman. I needed peace in my life. I had never known true peace before. I am writing this book to honour the Lord JESUS CHRIST, and to give glory to God the Father. I believe that God has given me another chance. I blew many chances before, but God has been gracious to me. I also believe that by reading this book God will enable many to receive healing and deliverance.

# CHAPTER 1

## IGNORANCE IS NO DEFENCE

Because of my ignorance, I almost perished.

KNOWLEDGE IS CHEAP BUT IGNORANCE IS COSTLY

There is an African saying that what you do not know will not kill you. I vehemently disagree. We, as responsible children of God need to be cognisant of the forces of evil that surround us. I have actually experienced first hand the incidents I have written about in this book. Now I am healed, delivered and set free from Satan's hold. Through the power of Jesus' blood I am now free indeed! Jesus Christ is my personal saviour – I am BORN AGAIN!!! To be born again, never again to suffer needlessly

I have observed that many individuals who claim to be born again go through many trials and tribulations. Some of the things happening may be because of ignorance and satan sure can take advantage of this ignorance. In other cases some will be reaping what they or their grandparents have sown. What I do know is that Jesus came that we may have life and life in abundance. Do you experience true joy in your life? Can you truly say that you are happy with your life and with your family life? If you are not, then you do not have life in abundance. Jesus himself said that he came that we might have life. We have to have that life in abundance.

(PSALM 124):
*If the Lord had not been on our side let Israel say;*
*If the Lord had not been on our side when men*
*attacked us, When their anger flared against us, they*
*would have swallowed us alive. The flood would*
*engulf us; the torrent would have swept over us. The*
*raging waters would have swept us away. Praise be to*

*the Lord who has not let us be torn by their teeth. We have escaped like a bird out of the fowler's snare, the snare has been broken, and we have escaped. Our help is in the name of the Lord, the maker of heaven and earth.*

I now realise that God has spared my life for His purpose and glory. I was not able to shield myself from the dangers and evil forces of this world. But God by His mercy, love and grace gave me another chance to live and enjoy life abundantly. Many times I failed because I did not give any thought to the living God. However, He had marvellous plans in store for me.

God says in His word in (Jeremiah 29:11-14):
*"For I know the plans I have for you", declares the Lord, "Plans to prosper you and not to harm you, plans to give you hope and a future. Then you will call upon me and pray to me, and I will listen to you. You will seek me and find me when you seek me with all your heart. I will be found by you," declares the Lord, "and I will bring you back from captivity. I will gather you from all the nations and places where I have banished you", declares the Lord, "and I will bring you back to the place from which I carried you into exile."*

I was once captive to Satan, but God brought back me to the place where He wanted me to be – having the right relationship with Him. And to be in his perfect will. Now I have found my purpose. It is like getting a precious pearl. When that happens you will sell everything so that you can purchase one precious pearl of value.

I was born in Zimbabwe, Africa. Its inhabitants indulge in ancestor worship. That is very normal and commonplace even among those who call themselves Christians. They believe that you communicate to God through your ancestors.

Many Christians in Africa intermix worship of God with ancestor worship. They have no qualms about indulging in both. That is normal to them. They see it as a matter of expediency.

If God works for them, let it be God. If ancestor worship works for them then so be it. It is quite common for people to go and seek the advice of the witchdoctors for any spiritual problem they may encounter.

The witchdoctor in turn will consult the spirits of their clients' ancestors in order to resolve their problems. Witchdoctors are held in high regard in certain societies in Africa. They are seen as problem shooters. Whenever a problem arises in the family they would seek the advice of the witchdoctors. But, whose power do these witch doctors use?

Whenever a family encounters difficulties, they would sit down together and decide on a plan of action. The elders make the final decision. Africans are very alert and conscious of the spiritual realm. They can discern when there is a spiritual problem in their lives and or the lives of their offspring. This will make the elders to look for help when certain things go wrong. They also advise each other accordingly. One can say, "I have a certain problem." The other would answer, "Friend, can't you see that your problems are not from the physical realm but from the spiritual? What you need to do is to go you need to go to a reliable witchdoctor and he should tell you what is wrong in your life."

That is how they solve the problems that afflict them. That was how their forefathers solved their problems and that is the way they solve them. Their children and their grand children are also taught to approach problems in this manner. This is passed on from generation to generation.

When you go to the witchdoctor you have to be prepared to pay for the consultation. No one goes to the witchdoctor empty-handed. It would be an insult to these people. The advice one gets from the witch doctor is much valued. He might for instance advise you to brew beer to appease the unhappy spirits, or sacrifice an animal, or things of that sort – things the spirits request you to do.

They are prepared to go through all that because that's what they sincerely believe in. it does not matter how stupid the advice from these people is they would still do it. An example is a child is not supposed to verbally or physically abuse a parent. When this happens it is supposed to bring dire consequences to the offending child. Later on in life when that offending person goes through some difficulties and they go to the mediums. They would be told of the offence that the individual did to the parent. In this case they are advised to hold a special ceremony of apologising to the parents. This is done weather the parent is dead or alive. The culprit has to dress in sackcloth and ashes. He goes round the community confessing the wrong that he has done. After this has been done he gets allowed into the family home. He takes off the sackcloth and gets washed in specially prepared water .and herbs. This is supposed to cleanse the individual of all the bad luck and problems that resulted from abusing one's parent.

I have seen well educated people do that I have seen so called Christians go to mediums and consulting the spirit of the dead. If you look in the word of God in exodus 20 on the Ten Commandments, the commandment with a promise is honour your father and your mother so that you may live long in the land that the lord your God is giving you. You see that satan is not original he copies all the things of Jehovah God and makes it his own.

The error is that these individuals do not realise that they are indulging in demon worship. They do not realise that they are giving honour to demons. They sincerely believe that this approach is the right one.

Usually individuals are encouraged to appease their ancestor spirits by doing whatever it takes to please them. Most responsible heads of families gather the families together at specific times to offer sacrifices to the gods and spirits of their families. They consult the advice of mediums for all the issues pertaining to family life. They like to know what will happen in the future and they like to be prepared for it.

In Africa, everybody belongs to a clan or a village. Every one is known by the name of their family of tribe. The elders of the families like to keep all the blood relations controlled in one way or the other. If a woman gives birth to any child these people do special rituals to make sure that the new born belongs to the clan. They have a fear of raising offspring that are not their own. Young people migrate to the towns find jobs there. Nevertheless, they ultimately return to their villages. That's where the bones of their ancestors lie. Their wealth and everything they consider sacred is in the village.

Elders always request the younger ones to bury them back in their villages where their ancestors lie buried. It does not matter where they die, they will always insist on being taken back to lie with their forefathers when the end comes. Some who live abroad insist on being taken to the village when the end comes. The remaining relations do whatever it takes to take the body back to the villages. Funerals are conducted in some specific ways. They have special rituals that are performed. The Africans fear and respect the dead more than the living. A person can be ill for some time. No one helps with the hospital bills or medicines. As soon as that person dies some relations do more for the dead than when the individual was living. They are aware of the consequence of not abiding with this custom.

In the spirit realm ancestors must be kept happy. There is no sorry in the worship of ancestors, rites have to be done in a special way and families would do whatever is necessary to see that this is so. If good fortune happens to an individual family - for example, one can buy a new car or a house or get a job or be promoted at work - they would pay homage to their ancestors for providing these amenities. They would pour a libation of beer and celebrate. As the elders pour libation on the car they say prayers of thanksgiving to the dead. It is a common belief that the dead are wiser and can hear the prayers of their relations. In turn these dead relations take these prayers to God. This is in direct contradiction to the Word of God. In (John 14:6) Jesus says, "I am the way, the truth and the life: no man cometh unto the Father, but by me." Any other way to God is wrong. Jesus is the only way to God in heaven.

When I was growing up I was ignorant of the ways of Jehovah God. No one in my family ever graced the inside of a church. I never liked nor trusted the Christians whom I knew. The ones with whom I was acquainted with were just as immoral as I was. They committed the same sins as I did. I had always imagined that church-going people were supposed to be moral and upright. But these acted contrary to the way Christians are supposed to behave.

At the time, I was not born again, but somehow I had had higher expectations of those who professed to be Christians. The practising Christians I knew used to drink alcohol gossip and commit all kinds of ungodly acts. I never met a good ambassador for Jesus then. This made me realise that those who are born again are constantly being watched and criticized by the non believers. These non Christians know more about the does and don'ts of God. They say things like I thought you were a Christian and you know Christians are not supposed to act like that. How have you been walking with Jesus? Are you a good ambassador for the Lord Jesus? Remember that others are watching and assessing you! You are a living testimony by choosing to walk the right way the holy way!

My grandparents on the paternal side were immigrants from Malawi. They did not teach us the ways of Jehovah God. They only knew what their forefathers had taught them, that is, ancestral worship, traditional healing and 'Gure wamukuru Zimbabwe.' The latter being a form of demon worships which involves masquerading and dancing all through the night. This is a very potent form of witchcraft, demon worship, and the occult.

Many people used to come for consultation at my grandparents' home. My grandfather was a well-known witch doctor who was much feared by other people. He expected people to move out of the way when he was passing by. No one went near him anyhow. They had to pay obeisance to him. He thought that he was a god. He called his house a mountain where people found solution to life.

He used to perform healings. Many testified about his amazing powers. I know for a fact that he did not use the name of Jesus. Jesus was not mentioned in my family. Those with spiritual problems whether it involved marriages, sexual dysfunction, financial problems, bad luck, bareness or demon possession used to consult my grandparents and he used to solve the problems for them

I remember when I was a little girl a woman came to seek help for her daughter whose breasts were growing on her back instead of her chest. Her family was at a loss as to why that had happened. They were of the opinion that witchcraft was to blame. My grand father healed her and she became normal! These people held him in high esteem. When he got his payment he would never accept the money directly from the hands of the people. He always had to call one of us his grand children to take the money for him. We would in turn put the money in a wooden plate. He would give thanks for the money then used it for whatever he wanted to do with it.

My Nan specialized in healing children. For example, those children whose fontanels had not fused on time. We were used to seeing these toddlers running around with black herbs on their fontanels. The fontanels would fuse after consultation with her. She specialised in healing those children who were dumb or slow to speak. I remember her making cuts under the children's tongues. After a while they would speak. You have to realize that in Africa they believe that if children are not well protected from evil a lot of bad happens to them.

Some physical problems have a natural scientific explanation, but most Africans tend to believe that the supernatural is responsible for many maladies. Some have a rational explanation but people are entitled to their own beliefs. Because of this some individuals would shell out their hard earned cash to the witch doctor. So you can see Satan and his agents certainly are able to heal.

Not all healing comes from God and not all healing is good. Some healing comes from Satan. In later chapters you will come to see how some of the things that my grandparents did affected my life in a negative way. I inherited these curses from them.

Some curses are passed on from generation to generation. Most problems that some children face are a result of what their Fore parents did. At times the problems have a modern twist to it.

My maternal grand parents were immigrants from Mozambique. They walked from Mozambique to Zimbabwe and they settled on a small farm in Selous. They were farm labourers who worked very diligently. To supplement their income my Nan used to brew beer. This is very common in Africa. The beer or spirit is very potent. A small drop will quickly make you drunk. It also damages your liver and is highly addictive. It is also illegal to brew it in Zimbabwe. In the vernacular language the beer is called kachasu or tototo and my Nan used to drink a lot of it. She also smoked cigars. Her husband, my granddad, was a carpenter and he made lots of money plying his trade. They, too, did not walk according to the precepts of God. They followed their ancestors' teachings. They gave honour to demonic spirits. They appeased the spirits of the dead and consulted mediums.

One of my cousins died when he was a baby. At his funeral they shaved off the hair of all the close relations and put it in a special calabash. My hair also was shaved. They mixed the hair with special herbs and concoctions and made a ceremony to the dead. In this particular family I noticed that many children died in their infancy. My eldest uncle's children also died as soon as they were born. My uncle got so fed up with the deaths he went to the witchdoctor to find out the reason for this occurrence. He was told that members of his family were doing some evil to him – by putting curses on his children.

Africans are very much aware of the reality of witchcraft. They know that evil spirits can attack and kill. Members of families that practice witchcraft take it in turn to kill members of each other's families. They believe that the witches kill human beings in order to devour their flesh and use it for evil rituals. It is only now that I have discovered that this killing of human beings is in reality sacrificing to Satan.

Many young women sacrifice to Satan nowadays by aborting their babies. I will call this sin what it is in plain language: MURDER OF THE UNBORN.

Over 26 million abortions are committed in the world today Medicine and science try to make it look innocent. It is not! The devil is still the same as in former times. He is just adjusting to the times. He is killing unborn babies in the name of science. Abortion is a sin and any woman who has committed an abortion is a murderer. And any man who has encouraged his wife, girlfriend, sister or anybody to terminate a pregnancy is also guilty of murder. The person who paid for the abortion and any doctor who has done this are just as guilty of murder. You need to renounce and repent of this sin for if you don't, you will pay for it. It is an abject violation of God's law which states that you must not murder.

In the Old Testament days they committed infanticide on a very large scale. They did this to appease the Babylonian goddess Ashtoreth. One of her devout worshippers was a queen named Jezebel. Next to the temple of Jezebel were the graves of thousands of infants. Jezebel had a palace containing jars of the remains of infants She believed they made her skin tender and delicate.

(Isaiah 47:1-15) reads:
*"Go down and sit in the dust, virgin daughter of Babylon, sit on the ground without a throne, Daughter, of the Babylonians, no more will you be called tender or delicate. Take millstones and grind the flour, take off your reads. Lift up your skirts. Bare your legs and wade through the streams. Your nakedness will be exposed and your shame uncovered. I will take vengeance I will spare no one. Our redeemer the Lord Almighty is His name-is the holy one of Israel. Sit in silence go into darkness Daughter of the Babylonians no more will you be called queen of the kingdoms. I was angry with my*

*people and desecrated my inheritance. I gave them into your hand,
and you showed them no mercy. Even on the aged, you laid a very
heavy yoke on them. You said, I will continue forever- the eternal
queen. But you did not consider these things or reflect on what might
happen. Now then you listen you wanton creature lounging in your
security, and saying to yourself, "I am and there is no one besides
me. I will never be a widow, or suffer loss of children. Both of these
will overtake you in a moment, on a single day. Loss of children and
widowhood will come upon you in full measure, in spite of your much
sorcery and all your potent spells. You have trusted in your
wickedness and have said no one sees me. Your wisdom and
knowledge mislead you when you say to yourself, I am and there is no
one besides me. Disaster will come upon you, and you will not know
how to conjure it away. A calamity will fall upon you that you
cannot ward off with a ransom. A catastrophe you cannot foresee
will suddenly come upon you. Keep on then with your magic spells
and with your much sorcery, which you have laboured at since
childhood. Perhaps you will succeed perhaps you will cause terror.
All the counsel you have received has only worn you out. Let your
astrologers come forward those stargazers who make predictions
month by month. Let them save you from what is coming upon you.
Surely they are like stubble the fire will burn them up. They cannot
even save themselves from the power of the flame. There are no coals
to warm anyone. There is no fire to sit by. This is all they can do
for you- those you have laboured with and trafficked with since
childhood. Each of them goes on in his error; there is not one that
can save you."*

As you can see, Jezebel was a rebellious woman who was a
practitioner of witchcraft and murder. That spirit is still operative now,
even in some marriages, and at the work place and even in some
churches.

Going back to my family, my uncle never asked who was casting an
evil spell in the family. He decided to move away and go and live
elsewhere. He now has children of his own. The sad thing is that one
of his daughters was murdered when she was nine. Apparently, she

was sexually molested and murdered by a paedophile. The murderer has not yet been caught and brought to justice.

Some strange phenomenon occurred in my maternal family. Many members were attacked by unusual maladies. Anytime one of them became ill, my Nan and aunts would consult the witchdoctors. One of my cousins went blind when she was thirteen and my Nan took her all the way to Mozambique to a powerful witchdoctor. She said this witchdoctor performed certain rites for her then, and that he even commented on her bravery. After the rites were over my cousin was healed, but she has encountered many other problems in her life.

We noticed that deaths in the maternal side of our family occurred in twos. The deaths usually occur after a spell of long illness and suffering. As I write this book one of my cousins has just died. Two days afterwards my Nan also passed away. This has happened in Zimbabwe, Africa. As soon as the family buried my cousin they had to go to another village to bury my Nan. Hospital fees, medicine and funerals are very expensive. I used to send lots of money to Africa for this. One way or the other something would happen that would make me spend money that I had worked so hard for. I had tons of unexpected bills. Whenever I acquired some money it ended up being used for something rather unexpected. The devourer used to have a field day with my finances. The above incident is indicative of what used to happen with my hard-earned money. We had to send money to help with unexpected expenses.

When I was discussing this with my husband he said that these were the demons of theft that were operating in my life. It was the spirit of poverty, it did not matter how much money I had, I would end up spending it on some emergency or the other. If you have a spirit of Poverty, you can lose a million pounds in a jiffy. You will not even be able to give an account on how you spent it. My money would just disappear from my hands.

(Malachi 3: 1-12) says:

*"I, the Lord do not change. So you O descendants of Jacob are not destroyed. Ever since the time of your forefathers you have turned away from my decrees and have not kept them. Return to me and I will return to you, says the Lord Almighty. But you ask how we to return are? Will a man rob God? Yet you rob me. But you ask how do we rob you? In tithes and offerings, you are under a curse- the whole nation of you- because you are robbing me. Bring the whole tithe into the storehouse, that they may be food in my house. Test me in this, says the Lord Almighty, and see if I will not throw open the floodgates of heaven and pour out so much blessings that you will not have room enough for it. I will prevent pests from devouring your crops and the vines in your fields will not cast their fruit, says the Lord Almighty. (Malachi 3:11) says, "And I will rebuke the devourer for your sakes and he shall not destroy the fruits of your ground."*

The devourer was really having a field day in my family. We were suffering because of the lack of knowledge. My grandparents were hard workers but they lived in poverty. I am now giving you some examples to enlighten you - you can try and figure out what is happening in your life. Do you have a very good job? Do you get paid well but still you do not see something constructive with your wages? Are you over qualified but do a menial job that is below your qualifications?

Or are you being turned down from certain jobs because you are over qualified? Do you find it difficult to get a job and are your finances being frittered away? It could be that you have to pay fines for your children who are in police custody. Or your own children steal from you to feed their drug habits. Then, do you frequent houses of prostitution and give all your earnings to the prostitutes? By the time you realize what has happened, you end up borrowing to get by to the next payday. Did you get robbed in the street or at home? When some men are in financial straits, they vow not to waste money like that again. However, when the next payday comes they will do the same, the cycle never ends - only Jesus can end that cycle! Let me leave the credit card and impulsive shopping alone. Do you go shopping and buy, buy, buy? When you get home you discover that you do not need all that you have just bought. How about buying lots of food and then throwing it in the bin because it has gone bad before you ate it.

What could be happening in your life? Only Jesus can rebuke the devourer for our sakes. I have had friends tell me that money literally disappears from their purses. How could that be? What is the devourer doing in your life? This is one curse, which you can readily get rid of by simply obeying what God says in His word. The most important thing to do when you receive your pay cheque is firstly to pay your tithes and offerings.

Those who patronise witchdoctors know that they cannot go to them empty-handed. Nevertheless, many Christians think nothing of going in the House of God without an offering. Now is the time for Satan to stop stealing from the children of God. We need to give to God what belongs to God and also to offer sacrifices for the upkeep of His House. How can we say we love God and do not even give to the maintenances of His House?

## HISTORY

My paternal grandparents used to relate folk stories to all their grandchildren. I used to love listening to their story telling, as most of the stories were very educative morally and culturally. I am certainly so delighted that they related to me tales of my ancestors and how they lived in their day. This gave me a good understanding of my roots. It also helped me in my deliverance. When I was renouncing the curses I knew what I was dealing with and was sure of what to renounce and steer clear from.

For example, my grandfather would warn us to look carefully at intersections when we walked on any intersection of small footpaths or large roads. A lot of charms would be thrown there during witchcraft rituals and some rituals that honoured ancestral rites. We used to sidestep those crossings whenever we saw any charms or anything suspicious at the crossings. We believed that if you walk carelessly whatever curse or hex was placed there, would attack you. Sometimes we would see blood, charms and dead animals that were placed at the intersection of the streets. We would side step them and say something that my granddad taught us to say when we encountered those things. Some people have encountered a lot of problems after stepping on those places.

Just to sidetrack a little, I was walking across the traffic lights near to my street in England. Something said to me "Look up!" I looked at the traffic lights. Lo and behold there was fresh blood on all the lights. I rebuked the curses that had been placed there in the name of Jesus. I pleaded the blood of Jesus over that particular area. From that day onwards I always pray for my street and ask God to intervene in every situation and circumstance in my neighbourhood when evil was at work.

# CHAPTER 2

## NO MORE SCAPEGOATS

My granddad dissuaded us from taking money from anybody. He informed us that money was used for witchcraft and if you accept it you will always have financial problems in your life. He told us of places where people went to throw money. He said that that money would be cursed. He discouraged us from picking money that was thrown on the streets. He said that most of it was used on some rituals or the other and that whoever picked it up would end up with demonic possession. Many of the things that had been there were not just by accident. Someone had deliberately placed them there and whoever picked them up would end up demon possessed. He taught us to be respectful to elders and not to be quarrelsome. He said that if you offend people they would get angry and put a curse on you.

He also insisted that we should be humble since proud individuals incur the wrath of some wicked people. These would in turn invoke a curse on the proud individual so that the proud would be humiliated and learn their lesson.

Granddad insisted that we steered well clear of some animals that were not herded. These animals had been used in rituals and my grandfather warned us. Witchdoctors still use these as animals scapegoat offerings. We would see beautiful pure black/white or red goats or sheep. He said not to approach these animals as they were full of evil spirits. I was amazed when I was reading the Bible to learn that what these people do is almost the same as what the priests in the Old Testament did for atonement offering in cases of murder.

(Leviticus Chapter 16 verses 20 – 26) states:
*"When Aaron has finished atonement for the most holy place, the tent of the meeting and the altar; he shall bring forward the live goat. He is to lay both hands on the head of the live goat and confess over*

*it all the wickedness and the rebellion of the Israelites- all their sins and put them on the goat's head. He shall send the goat away into the desert in the care of a man appointed for the task. The goat will carry on itself all their sin to a solitary place. And the man shall release it in the desert. Then Aaron is to go into the tent of meeting and take off the linen garments he put on before he entered the most holy place and put on his regular garments. Then he shall come out and sacrifice the burnt offering for himself and the burnt offering for the people.*

*He shall also burn the fat of the sin offering on the altar, Verse 26 says, "the man who releases the goat as a scapegoat must wash his clothes and bathe him with water, afterwards he may come into the camp."*

The devil tries to counterfeit everything that God in heaven does. Now there is absolutely no need for any atonement by animals now that Jesus has sacrificed Himself for us through His blood and death on the cross. Jesus said on the cross, "It is finished!"

As I mentioned before my granddad warned us not to go near to the animals as they had been tainted with evil. We were aware that the families that had a lot of trouble would go to consult witchdoctors. The witchdoctors would in turn advise them - it could be that they should buy a goat or any other animal as a sacrifice. The family would then take the animals back to the witchdoctor. One animal would be killed and the blood sprinkled on the family. The witchdoctor in turn would lay hands on the other animal and perform certain rituals. The family would tell the witch doctor about the problems that were plaguing them. The witchdoctor would then transfer the problems into the live animal. This was supposed to get rid of the evil influences that were disturbing the family. Then they would take the goat to the forest, and let it loose there. They would then walk fast or run back to their home being careful not to look back.

When they arrived home they would wash their bodies with special concoctions given to them by the witchdoctor. This was supposed to be a form of cleansing. They were informed that if they looked back the problem would return back to them. The spiritual problems that they are facing would was supposed to be borne by the animal. Many Africans are aware that if the problem they are having is physical they know where to go for assistance. If it is a spiritual problem they also know where to go for help.

Sometimes thieves would steal the goat and either kill it for food or sell it to an unsuspecting victim. After the animal is slaughtered the spirit would be transferred to the one who has killed it and to those who had eaten its flesh. In this way many people would end up with insurmountable problems. And they would have had absolutely no idea where these problems came from.

If you are a thief, be careful what you steal, as some of the things that you steal can actually harm you. Someone will be mocking you and laughing at you in the spirit world. During my youth I was always aware of things like that. My granddad would warn us not to eat food that was offered to us by a stranger as that food would be the means whereby evil forces would be transferred to us. My Nan would give us (girls) special beads to wear on our waists. Maybe you have seen pictures of African women wearing these beads. They have special reasons to wear them.

While I was writing this book, I was having a conversation with my husband on the phone. He told me that a certain man was going to offer me some sweets and that that man meant to harm me. A week later I went to church and a certain parishioner offered me some chocolate. I refused the chocolate, but he insisted that I take it. I remembered what the man of God told me and so I still refused it. I could see the disappointment on the man's face. The following week the same man kept following me after the church service and was offering to buy me a drink. I refused the drink and asked him never to offer me anything to eat again. I would be careful whom I eat from because not everyone who attends church is right with God. The church is a public venue - everybody goes there, the good, the bad and the profane. Some people who go there are genuinely looking for help from God but some go there to cause strife and dissension among the congregation.

# CHAPTER 3

## FROM MALAWI TO ZIMBAWE

### THE LONG WALK TO RHODESIA  NOW  ZIMBABWE

My paternal grandparents related to us how they journeyed to Zimbabwe from Malawi. They told us about their grandparents and their great- great grandparents. Apparently my grandfather's great grandfather was one of the individuals who fled from Chaka Zulu the great king of Southern Africa. They are very powerful and cunning warriors called the Zwangendaba. These were the warriors who fought off Chaka Zulu using some very clever tactics. During a certain encounter with Chaka Zulu they managed to conquer him by throwing rocks and missiles at his troops from a high plateau. The tribe had to flee from South Africa to the north because Chaka Zulu was a well-known great warrior who had a powerful army. He could reorganise himself and defeat his enemies. So they fled north of South Africa and settled in Malawi. This tribe pierces big holes in their ears. Both men and women put big thick earrings in their ears. The tribe is also known for painting their bodies and casting hexes. It is a well-known fact that if you want strong witchcraft you go to Malawi to these elders.

My granddad would tell us about his father's sister who was well known as a great healer. When he was getting ready to migrate to Zimbabwe, this aunt took him aside and taught him her secrets. She gave him potions and various materials and initiated him. I am convinced that that was how he inherited the witchcraft. He always spoke very fondly of his aunt. He encouraged us to get closer to our aunts so that they too could teach us their secrets. He said when he left Malawi the elders commissioned him to take nothing for the journey except his wife, spear, and certain potions that the aunt had given him. With them they walked the long journey from Malawi to Zimbabwe some time between 1900 and 1930.

I remember him saying that in 1914 when he was between 6 to 10 years old, he remembered his dad going to fight in World War I. He died in 1995 when he was between 88 and 94. I do not know his real age.

## THE MIGRATION

He said that they meaning my nan and him walked from one country to another for a long time. When they sun had set and they could go no further. They had to rest and settle for the night. Because of some principalities in the spirit they did not settle any how. They had to follow a special procedure in order to appease the ruling spirits of that forest.

Most of you who come from Africa know that there are evil forests. No one goes in and out of these forests carelessly. If you do that there are dire consequences sometimes death. So in order to survive these evil forests you have to follow their way of doing things, or you have to be a very anointed servant of God and go the with the permission of God himself. So the grandparents knew these rules. They had to find a special tree. The rituals he did had to be done under that special tree only and it had to be the baobab tree .I do not know how they identified the right tree but he was a man with a lot of spiritual insight.

They would set up a special altar to pay homage to the rulers of that forest and to pray to their ancestors. This convinces me that some forests and trees that are cursed and are used by Satan's agents for evil purposes.

So before they settled for the night they would converse with ruling spirits of that land. This was done so that these spirits in the forests where he was at that time would not be offended by their trespassing. The rulers of those forests guard their things jealously

The conversation would go something like this: "We are foreigners in this land. Please do not be upset with us as we are just passing through your land. It's now dark, so please let us stay for the night. We will take all our belongings with us when it is day light."

It sounds like he had to beg the Prince of that place to remain there for the night. We are aware that every area has its own ruling Prince. For example, The Prince of Persia who delayed the angel that was sent to Daniel Read this in the book of Daniel. He would then summon his own ancestral spirits and say, "Our fore fathers, please protect and provide food and all we need for this journey as your children." As they speak, they would be kneeling down and clapping their hands. He said that after a while, hot food would appear from nowhere; they would eat and be satisfied. All their needs for the journey will be provided for. Also no harm from wild animals came their way. When they made the full journey they were in good health, no diseases in their bodies. Probably some innocent person would be cooking and serving her food. Then the food will just disappear from the table.

I figured out that many people lose money and things and they wonder what will have happened to their belongings. The demons of theft will have stolen from them and given it to their worshippers - the Devourer, the thief Satan steals it). Also it makes me realise that Satan looks after his own for a season even though he is only interested in stealing, killing and destroying. He gives his followers what they want for a season. He is the master of deception. When Satan takes back from his people he takes more than he gave because it is his nature to kill, steal and destroy.


ARRIVAL IN HARARE

When my paternal grandparents arrived in Harare Zimbabwe, they worked very hard and became very rich. My granddad owned a farm and was very wealthy for a season. My grandmother used to brew traditional beer and sell it and she also made lots of money from doing this. She used to put the money in tins and hide it in the ground but the money would disappear, so in that way she lost a lot of her wealth.

# CHAPTER 4

## LITTLE PRINCESS

### MY NAMING CEREMONY

When I was born I was given my grandmother's name. I did not know why they called me grandmother, as I was still very young. Later in this book you will find out that I was indeed possessed with the spirit of an old woman. That spirit made me age very quickly. I went into premature menopause at the age of twenty-four. I looked very old and behaved like an old woman. I would think twice now before I give my child a name, especially that of a dead or living relative.

I was a favourite grandchild and got away with anything. I always got preferential treatment and I revelled in it. I was brought up by my grandparents. My mom told me that when I was born my grandparents and aunts would literally be fighting to have the honour of raising me. It was like who ever got me first would get me for the day. As a baby they would take me with them everywhere. My grandparents loved to go to the public houses or bars to drink and to socialise, so I was all over the pubs with them. I would return to my mum in the evenings.

### TRADITIONAL DANCES:

As I grew up, I got to learn about the masquerade dancers whom I shall explain about later. My granddad was the top boss in these things. He ran them and organised them. He encouraged us to know about that way. He wanted us to keep the way, to teach it to our children and for our children to teach the way of our ancestors to their children. One of my cousins became an expert of the special drums. My granddad expected him to inherit his powers. it was not to be. However, he later died a painful and horrible death. He was very young when he died.

I came to learn that this was a cult and that my granddad was the head of it. He referred to himself as a god. He thought he was a mountain and every one in the village had to come and pay obeisance to him. He was very rich but later he became bankrupt. He was a very tough and cruel man. He was also intelligent and never drank or smoked. I now realise that he was at the top rank of this cult and always had to be alert. If he ever got in a drunken state there was always the possibility that someone would kill him. His position was coveted and someone was ready to step into his shoes. He could not afford to be careless. So literally ever so often there would be a dance somewhere and we would go with him. We loved going to these dances.

At these dances the masquerades always wore their masks, nobody knew who was behind the mask - they would be naked except for the clay paint on their bodies. Some would be wearing little grass skirts to cover the private parts but mostly the nakedness will be showing. I did not know that nakedness is a form of witchcraft. I will talk about the demonic altars in the later chapters.

### These dancers are greatly feared in Zimbabwe - everybody knows.

There is something eerie about these dancers. Whenever people talked about them they would advise each other not to approach any one of them at all. The people believed that these masquerades would murder you. They also encouraged each other to flee from them. These people also believed that if you fell down while fleeing from them, the wound you got would never heal as long as you lived. Your life would start going downhill too. In this cult there is a lot of jealousy and witchcraft. The members fight to get to the top ranks of their cult. People die mysteriously and the members are buried in special ways and special ceremonies and dances are held for them.

Some mothers who belonged to this group would willingly take their little children to these masquerades to be dedicated to the ancestors for they considered it to be a blessing. I was dedicated in this way. Most children are initiated and dedicated in this way and grow up with many problems plaguing their lives. At times they do not have an idea of where the problems originated from. Some of them would join the cult and follow ways of their fathers; life would be fine for a time then it would go bad later. There are those who do not follow the way of their ancestors or worship God. They just live anyhow. They do not know Jesus. They belong to no cult. They say that they were modern. But look out! These eventually have to confront many unexplained problems.

I now realise that one does not just exist. You have to serve Jesus and follow his ways and He will take your burdens and make them light. Or you have to serve Satan and he will take you to hell with him. As for me, I was obviously groomed in that way. How ignorant I was, how far from God my grandparents were!

(Hosea4:6): *"My people are destroyed from lack of knowledge."*
Up to now I do not blame my grand parents for what they did to me because they did not know better. Most Africans only know the ancestral way of worship and it works for them for a while. Thank God for the missionaries who are bringing the good news of the saving power of Jesus to Africa! Now Africa is changing

My grandparents longed to have a successor to carry on their tradition so they made sure that all males in the family were initiated. They had this done whether the boys liked it or not. On special dance days the masquerades would pounce on the young boys who had come of age and belonged to the tribe or family. They would then take them to a special secret place and initiate them into the secrets of the clan. Some boys would resist and run away from home for a few days. They ended up being caught and being forcefully initiated.
These masquerades used the power of witchcraft to catch them. They would march in a single file to where ever the boys would have gone to. They would paralyse the boys by the power of witchcraft. By the time they finished the initiation the boys would be so subdued and they will be very loyal to the masquerades. We used to ask some of my

close cousins what happened to them. They would never reveal anything. Whatever happened there they were sworn to secrecy.

Women were not allowed to witness these ceremonies as they were only for men. The girls had a different form of initiation when they came of age. They call it "pulling". The girls would be taken away to a special place and taught how to be women. In some cultures they circumcise the clitoris. In my culture they do the "pulling". There are also some special mothers who teach you how to do it. If you do not do it the right way they will beat you mercilessly. It's a physically abusive ritual where special herbs and concoctions are used .to initiate you. If you do not have that done you are not considered to be a real woman.

There is another initiation that is done for girls only. A special feast is held for a girl who has started menstruating. The elders gather at her parent's home all night. They eat and dance and they have an enjoyable time. A select group of women then take the young girl to a private bedroom. There they give her information relating to her menstrual cycle and what to do when she gets married. What goes on in that room is vulgar. Most women who had this done end up with a being who controls them. - a "spirit husband" They may marry and have lots of grief and heartache during their marriage. Some never marry at all. This spirit being believes he owns these women he pays the women or men norctunal visits and has sex with them in the dream. He blocks their chances of a happy marriage.

Others become very promiscuous or they would adopt a life-style that people would abhor. Many of these women do not talk about what they endure because it is a shameful and painful thing to go through. All my aunts and cousins had this procedure done to them.

HOW CAN YOU BE PROTECTED FROM EVIL?

Many Africans believe in demon possession. They believe that not all possession is bad. If you are a medium or a custodian of some family spirits. You are considered to be blessed. They say the spirit that is in you helps the community. Some mediums heal the sick. Hold the community together and all the things they believe that they are good for the family. Some evil possession is the one that use witchcraft and they damage the community. They also believe that if you are possessed with a bad spirit it can be cast out of you. The one with a good spirit can do that. They are very aware of the spiritual realm and of the existence of evil spirits. They consult the witchdoctor and have demonic healing, hence it is very easy for an African to believe in supernatural healing and have faith in the Evil One. They do not realise that they are in error. For that reason they go to all lengths to try to ward off evil by indulging in different rituals.

When a woman is pregnant she is given potions to prevent a miscarriage. After birth, the baby is bathed in various concoctions while some words are spoken over the life and future of that child.

Another ritual involves taking you to a special place like a river or a forest or somewhere very privatee. They strip you naked and cut your body at various strategic places with a razor blade. They then rub in traditional medicines into these cuts. You never know what it is that they are rubbing into you. I never knew until I was born again! I was not aware that they rubbed nasty things like snakeskin that had been burnt and grounded, and also other animal parts, and other horrible things I do not even want to mention.

These were meant to protect you from witchcraft attacks, evil eye, jealousy, bad luck and everything evil that can befall you. Most Africans are cut in this way. Some cuts are so small that they do not leave scars. But others are visible. Witches can cut you against your will and this will be explained in one of the chapters. A lot of herbs and potions were given to us to drink or used for steaming our bodies for the healing of most ailments and to rub on the body for protection against evil. This obviously opened doorways to demonic entrance.

When I was growing up life was very smooth for me. I lacked nothing. I also had no major health problems. I had a nice family, my grandparents treated me like a princess – how they adored me!

Before I went to the interview to train as a nurse I had to consult my elders first who made sure that I had potions of herbs under my tongue that were supposed to give me good luck. It was also supposed to confuse the interviewer so that he would give me a good report whether he thought so or not.

This gave me a lot of confidence as I believed in it totally. I got selected the very day of the interview and that enhanced my belief in the ancestral help.

# CHAPTER 5

## LITTLE PRINCESS BECOMES A NURSE.

I went to train as a nurse in a hospital that is quite a long distance from home. When I was in my second year of nursing I got involved with my first husband. We planned to get married after I had finished my nurse's training. It did not work out like that. We had a child out of wedlock. We decided to get married in a traditional marriage ceremony. It is an African custom for the man to pay a certain dowry to the wife's parents. He had to pay another special fine for making me pregnant before we got married. All this was done and we were legally husband and wife. This is a very acceptable thing to us as Africans. But in fact according to the law of God this was a violation of God's Word.

The Word of God says in (Deut 22:13-21):

*"If a man takes a wife and after lying with, dislikes her and slanders her and gives her a bad name, saying I married this woman but when I approached her I did not have proof of her virginity, the girl's father and mother shall bring proof that she was a virgin to the town elders at the gate, the girl's father will say to the elders I gave my daughter to this man but he dislikes her. Now he has slandered her and said "I did not find your daughter to be a virgin, but here is the proof of my daughter's virginity. Then the parents shall display the cloth before the elders of the town, and the elders shall take the man and punish him. They shall fine him a hundred shekels of silver and give them to the girl's father because this man has given an Israelite virgin a bad name. She shall continue to be his wife. He must not divorce her as long as he lives. If however the charge is true and no proof of the girl's, virginity can be found she shall be brought to the door of her father's house and there the men of her town shall stone her to death. She has done a disgraceful thing in Israel by being promiscuous while still in her father's house. You must purge the evil from among you."*

Despite marrying the same man after the incident, I had nevertheless committed a grievous sin. When you get married you become one with your partner. In the spiritual realm it is the same. There is no boyfriend and girlfriend in the spirit realm. You inherit the spiritual blessings or curses that your partner possesses. They inherit yours too. So if your spouse is cursed then you receive his curses yours and your life gets miserable. If you are blessed he inherits your blessing and also you give him/her your blessing. Have you ever noticed some people marry into blessed families and life gets so much better for them, the ones who marry into cursed families have their lives ruined by reason of marriage? Take for example, Israel had a king called Ahab son of Omri. He was one of the most wicked and most powerful of the kings of Israel in his time. He married Jezebel, a Sidonian princess through whose influence the worship of Baal of Asherah was established in Israel. She attempted to exterminate the prophets of Jehovah God. She had evil influence over Ahab. She had Naboth killed for his own vineyard.

Also, there was a good king of Judah called Jehoshaphat he had a son called Jehoram. In (2 Kings 8:18), it says that Jehoram walked in the ways of the kings of Israel, as the house of Ahab had done, for he married a daughter of Ahab. He did evil in the eyes of the Lord.

Who are you married to that the Lord sees it as doing evil in His eyes?

This is how the family of Ahab and Jezebel was cut off. (2 Kings 10:1-17) says:

> "Now there were in Samaria seventy sons of Ahab. So Jehu wrote letters to the officials of Jezreel, to the elders and to the guardians of Ahab's children. He said since your master's sons are with you and you have chariots and horses, a fortified city and weapons. Choose the best and most worthy of your master's sons and best him on his fathers throne. Then fight for your master's house. But they were terrified and said if two kings could not resist him, how can we? So the palace administrator, the city governor the elders and the guardians sent this message to Jehu. "We are your servants and we

*will do anything you say. We will not appoint anyone as king; you do what ever you think best." Then Jehu wrote them a second letter, saying, "if you are on my side and you obey me, take the heads of your masters sons and come to me in Jezreel by this time tomorrow." Now the royal princes seventy of them were with the leading men of the city, who were rearing them. When the letter arrived, these men took the princes and slaughtered them. They put their heads in a basket and sent them to Jehu in Jezreel. When the messenger arrived, he told Jehu, 'they have brought the heads of the princes'. Then Jehu ordered, put them in two piles at the entrance of the city gates until morning.*

*The next morning Jehu went out. He stood before the people and said, 'you are innocent. It was I who conspired against my master and killed him, but who killed all these? Know then that not a word the Lord has spoken against the house of Ahab will fail. The Lord has done what he promised through his prophet Elijah.' So Jehu killed everyone in Jezreel who remained of the house of Ahab, as well as all his chief men, his priests leaving him no survivors. Jehu set out and went towards Samaria. At Beth-Eked of the Shepard's he met the relatives of Ahaziah king of Judah and asked who are you? They said we are relatives of Ahaziah we have come down to greet the families of the king and queen mother.*

*Take them alive he ordered. So they took them alive and slaughtered them by the well of Beth-Eked, forty-two men. He left no survivors. After he left there he came upon Jehonadab son of Rehab who was on his way to meet him. Jehu greeted him and he said, "Are you in accord with me, as I am with you?" "I am", Jehonadab answered. If so give me your hand. So he did and Jehu helped him up into his chariot. Jehu said, come with me and see my zeal for the Lord. Then he had him ride along his chariot. When Jehu came to Samaria he killed all who were left there of Ahab's family. He destroyed them according to the word of the Lord spoken to Elijah."*

According to the above passage several innocent people were slaughtered by reason of marriage or friendship, relations of an old evil king and Queen, Ahab and Jezebel.

# CHAPTER 6

## THE SPIRIT OF SHAME

What has been declared over your immediate family and your extended family? What lineage do you originate from? A lot of people suffer because of the sins of their ancestors. Mixing with wrong company can also bring you curses. Some people can be at the wrong place at the wrong time. Take for instance the case of Jonah.

Jonah (1:3 – 16) states:

> *"But Jonah ran away from the Lord and headed for Tar shish. He went down to Joppa, where he found where he found a ship headed for that port. After paying the fare, he went aboard and sailed for Tar shish to flee from the Lord. Then the Lord send a great wind on the sea, and such a violent storm arose that the ship threatened to break up. All the sailors were afraid and each cried to his own god. And they threw the cargo into the sea to lighten the ship. But Jonah had gone below the deck, was he lay down and fell into a deep sleep. The captain went to him and said. How can you sleep? Get up and call on your God. May be he will take notice of us, and we will not perish. Then the sailors said to each other, 'come let us cast lots to find out who is responsible for this calamity.' They cast lots and the lots fell on Jonah. So they asked him," tell us, who is responsible for making all this trouble for us? Where do you come from? What is your country? What do you? From what people are you?" He answered, "I am a Hebrew and I worship the Lord, the God of heaven, who made the sea and the land." This terrified them and they asked? What have you done? (They knew he was running away from the Lord because he had already told them so). The sea was getting rougher and rougher. So they asked him, "What should we do to make the sea calm down for us?" "Pick me up and throw me into the sea, he replied, and it will become calm. I know that it is my fault that this great storm has come upon you." Instead the men did their best to row back to land. But they could not because the*

*sea grew wilder than before. Then they cried to the Lord, "O Lord please do not let us die for taking this man's life. Do not hold us accountable for killing an innocent man, for you O Lord, have done as you pleased." Then they took Jonah and threw him overboard, and the raging sea grew calm. At this the men "greatly feared the Lord and made vows to him."*

My point is that in innocence the sailors, without any fault of their own, had the wrong results because they were in the wrong company aboard. Jonah went on their ship when they accepted Jonah on their voyage. Because they had Jonah on board they lost all their valuable cargo. They were in the company of a rebel so they lost their livelihood because they happened to be in the wrong company.

Is there a Jonah in your ship? What kind of friends do you have? What has gone wrong or right since you became friends, what has happened to you since you married your spouse?

The only good thing that came from it is as (verse 16) says. "At this the men greatly feared the Lord and they offered a sacrifice to the Lord and made vows to him."

I would be selective as to the friends I keep. Some company can bring death as you see with what happened in the scripture. Also some jobs are a death trap. Look at what happened to the people who were rearing the kings' sons. First they turned on the King's sons and cut off their heads. What kind of loyalty is that? They thought by doing that they would be safe but in the end they were killed. They murdered the ones who they were supposed to protect. I am sure they had thought that they would save their own skins. Look at how it ended!

WRONG COMPANY PRODUCES WRONG RESULTS

Now is the time to break those curses. Our Lord Jesus became a curse for us by being hung outside the camp on a tree so that we might be blessed. When you are cursed you may marry a very nice partner but the marriage will never last. You will always have problems with your partner. Something has to happen that will make you leave or kick your partner out.

By the time you come to your senses the damage will already have been done. Your partner will either hate you so much that he or she would not want to see you or you will be so afraid of your partner that you will not want to return to them. When you try to reconcile there could be a big blockade and you will never understand why. You could still probably love each other very much but it gets harder and harder to get back together. In some cases a cursed man will attract a cursed woman and they marry. A very good man who is cursed can marry an evil woman. The woman will torture the man so bad that the man cannot handle it. He would end up leaving the marital home. It can be visa versa. A cursed person cannot last in any relationship! I have noticed that a lot of bad things happen to good people, and a lot of men suffer abuse in the marital home. It is easy for a woman to cry and talk of domestic abuse but it is very hard for men to say, "Now I am no longer biased. I am aware that anyone can be abused."

Again, Satan can set up good Christian couples and attack their marriage. The agents of Satan torture these Christians endlessly. Satan hates marriage and he will do anything to split the family unit. He likes the pain confusion and trauma that comes from a broken home. I suggest to all who know our God Jehovah not to marry out of the will of God. We need to be equally yoked and not mix with darkness. In our church we get our partners approved by the Holy Spirit.

The archbishop and the pastors in the church where I worship called off many engagements that were not right in the eyes of God. When these cancellations are done. It is a very painful thing to begin with. In the end the people find out something about their former fiancee that shocks them. They always come back and give God the glory for being spared. I noticed that those who marry in the will of God never get divorced. The only divorcees in our Church are those who joined the congregation after they were divorced. As soon as they understand what has happened in their marriages, they deal with their issues in the way that God prescribes. They either have their marriages restored by God or the person moves on. I have seen a lot of marriages being restored.

I married into a family that did not know God. They did all kinds of abominations that were not pleasing in the God's eyes. They sought the advice of spiritualists. I was in agreement with them as that was the only way I knew. The father of my first husband died before I met him. He lost all his riches before he died. They say that he was a very wealthy polygamous businessman. The children from the different mothers did not get on at all. They were very suspicious of each other. They did their ancestral dances secretly. They did not consult their stepbrothers. As a daughter- in- law, I was told how bad the other family was. I was never introduced to them. They believed that all their problems were the result of the witchcraft done by the family of the other woman.

As I write this book all the sons in that family but one are dead. That includes my first husband. We had divorced by the time he died. He did very well in his short life. He reached to the peak of his career. Life was going very well for him and suddenly he died. The doctors say that it was pneumonia. The wife that he married after we had divorced died 10 days after him. I was so grateful to God that I was divorced from him by the time that he died. Or else who knows? I would have been dead too. All the sons of the family are dead. They seemed to do very well for a season then they suddenly passed away. That is a pattern of a curse right there. When they reach their peak they die suddenly. The daughters are widowed at a very young age. The grandmother is left with about thirteen grandchildren. Her sons and their wives are dead. At her old age she has to fend for these children. She has to send them to school and do all that needs doing to raise the young ones. My daughter is the only one with a parent.

MARRIAGE NUMBER ONE

My mother in law disliked me and that feeling was mutual. She literally manipulated my marriage and turned my ex-husband against me. I found that very hard to take. Each time she came to visit our home she would engender strife. We were at each other's throat like animals. Something would happen that would make him violent towards me and I would reciprocate. At the instigation of his mother, my ex-husband would suddenly turn violent towards me and I would retaliate. When she was around we were at each other's throat like a pack of wild animals. I was normally calm, but as soon as my mother-in-law appeared things changed for the worse and that was not good for the marriage.

The last straw was her last visit to our home. I believe she came to intentionally destroy our marriage. I was in bed sleeping and my mother-in-law was talking to my spouse in the lounge. He forthwith angrily stalked into the bedroom and started shouting and screaming at me. Then he started to hit me. I just lost my temper. I locked the bedroom door and started fighting back. I summoned up unusual strength and I beat him up so badly that he fractured his hand. I did not know at the time where that strength came from. only Now do I know that that strength was demonic. I am quite small in stature but I was able to overpower him. How I did so, I do not know.

When you grow up in certain African families, at a certain time, the elders cut you with a razor and put different medications within these cuts for various purposes. One reason is to give you strength to be able to fight. My aunts used to say to me never let a man hit on you. You have to fight back. They were good fighters themselves. They had me cut wit a razor and had special portions of herbs rubbed into the cuts. This was to enable you to fight.

I never started up a fight. That was not my nature. How ever my belief was if you stared it I had to finish it. In this instance after I had beaten up my ex-husband, my mother-in-law came into the room to try and make peace. When I saw her face I remembered all the bad things she had said and done to me. I thought I would pay her back for all that. So I gave her also a sound thrashing. They were shaken.
That done I jumped over a high fence and went to a friend's house. The friend then took me to my parent's home.

When I reached my parent's home, I told them what had happened to me. I told my dad an exaggerated version of what had happened. I said to my dad that my ex husband and all his family had ganged on me and beat me up. Dad was very annoyed to hear what had occurred. He said he was going to call all my cousins so they could go and fight with the ex husband and his family. One of my saner uncles managed to calm down everyone.

I was very bitter and broken hearted. I did not understand what had happened. At one minute I was in my bed going to sleep, the next I was fighting with him. And now I am thinking of divorce. How did it get to here so quick?

I decided then and there to get a divorce. My husband tried to persuade me to return to the marital home, but I steadfastly refused. I was taught that once a man lays a hand on a woman the first time then do not give him another opportunity to repeat it. I believe that it would happen over and over again. I have seen a lot of domestic violence in my life. I have seen women being disfigured by men and vice versa. I thought to myself I might end up either killing him or he would do the same to me. So I talked of having a divorce right away. I now realize that I was right to turn my back on him. He died ten years later and the woman he later married died a week after him. I always think that it could have been me who would have died. God protected me from the curse that was killing the sons and wives of that family.

Incidentally, before the break-up, I visited my grand father. As I mentioned before he was a well-known and respected witchdoctor. As every elder will do, he was questioning me about the state of my marriage. I was complaining to him that my mother-in-law was interfering in my marriage. He then gave me a potion of herbs and said that when I return home I should mix this with my floor polish and polish the floor with it. He said that that portion of herbs would confuse anyone who wanted to interfere with my marriage. I did as he instructed me. Instead of the marriage getting stronger it got worse. I could not figure out why the potion had not done what it was supposed to do. I then lost confidence in the witchdoctors. They had not helped in my marriage.

I did not seek the help of the Lord; instead, I sought the help of man. That helped to destroy my marriage! Anyone who seeks the help of man instead of God is cursed! (Judges 5:23) says, "Curse Meroz, said the Angel of the Lord, curse its people bitterly because they did not come to the help of the Lord, to the help the Lord against the mighty."


## THE FIRST DIVORCE

In my country divorce is something that is looked down upon. The woman is usually blamed for being the guilty partner. Regardless of the circumstances it's always the woman who is expected to stick it out. I could not remain in that marriage as I mentioned before. I was so mad and did not believe that there was hope for the marriage. I do not believe in abusing anyone – verbally or physically. So the shame of the divorce was following me.
It drove me to work very hard so I could achieve better things. I had all the material things that I could hope for. This did not fill the empty void in my heart. I tried to drown my sorrows with alcohol. When I woke up the emptiness was still there. Alcohol just temporarily eased my pain. I tried visiting clubhouses and partying but nothing helped. I travelled to the most beautiful places in the earth. Nothing was good for me. I tried to go to a white garment church. No help. I knew the pain and the sorrow that was in my heart. It was a shameful thing for me. I could not share it with anyone.

I did not know about Jesus and his Word. In (Matt 11: 28-30), Jesus says, "Come to me, all you who are weary and burdened, and I will give you rest. Take my yoke upon you and learn from me, for I am gentle and humble in heart, and you will find rest for your souls. For my yoke is easy and my burden is light."

I did not know Jesus could help!

# THE DREAMS AND VISIONS

I used to dream amazing dreams and see funny visions.

One day I dreamt that a big long snake was leading me to a far away country. When I woke up, I told this to one of my elder aunts at home. She said to me that my ancestors were leading me to a good country and that all will be well with me there. I forgot all about the dream but I only remember as I am writing this book. THE SNAKE IS SATAN HIMSELF {Rev 12:9-17}. That meant that I was dreaming of Satan himself. I was dreaming of the devil himself. He was leading me in the ways that I should go. If you dream of snakes it is not good. It is the spirit of Satan himself. Usually a lot of trouble comes after dreams like that. When I was going through deliverance I got rid of all the snake prints in my house. I used to like some clothes and shoes with snake patterns on them.

Some people like to wear clothes with a dragon and snakes on them. These people do not realise that in doing so they open a doorway for the snake spirit to enter into to their lives. (Revelation 12:7-9) says, "And war broke out in heaven, Michael and his angels fought against the dragon. The dragon and his angels fought back, but they were defeated, and there was no longer a place for them in heaven. The great dragon was thrown down, that ancient serpent, which is called the devil and Satan, the deceiver of the whole world - he was thrown to the earth, and his angels were thrown down with him."

So this is really who Satan is. He cannot do you good in your dream or in your daily life!

Some dreams come from Satan and he tells you exactly what to do. The dreams that come from God do not confuse you. If you are a dreamer, you need to know which dreams are from God and which are from Satan. Satan can programme your mind and he can manipulate you in your dreams. When I was having these dreams I used to be so happy because I thought that my ancestors were in touch with me and they were leading me. I had no idea that you go to God only through his only begotten son Jesus Christ. At the time I only knew that sort of worship, which is ancestral worship. A lot of Africans believe that you should stick to what works for you. For a season this worked well for me. I was blinded to the gospel. A lot of people used to tell me about Jesus, I listened to them but never understood what they were trying to tell me.

# CHAPTER 7

## FROM ZIMBABWE TO ENGLAND

### THE BIG MOVE TO ENGLAND

Somehow I decided to go to England. I thought that this new country where nobody knew me would be a good starter to a different life. I thought that if I moved, my problems would be over. Little did I know that if you are demonised or cursed the spirits will follow you wherever ever you go. These things do not go away just because you have changed location

When I told my dad that I wanted to move and live in England, he was so pleased. They sat down with the elders of the family so that they would have a special party for me. This was of course, a ritual. They would prepare a party with food and all that goes along with it. The bottom line is that they also had to brew traditional beer and do what was supposed to be done in order to appease the ancestors. I invited all my friends and neighbours. Did we have a party! Quite implorable! After everyone left, my close relatives performed the ritual for me to ensure that I would have a safe travel to London. I felt protected. My journey to London was uneventful. It was easy for me to get a job, as I am a trained nurse.

I used to live in the nurses' home with some Christian girls. They were always so happy and good to me. Their salvation was evident in their day-to-day walk. One example was a Nigerian lady named Joke, whom I loved and admired for being a real woman of God, living at peace with everyone and whose life exhibited all the fruits of the Spirit. I was curious as to why the Christian girls were different from everyone else I knew. They had something about them. What was it? I even asked one of the girls why she was so happy and peaceful all the time and she replied that it was the presence of Jesus in her life.

I could not believe that Jesus could transform a person's life to be so good! I said to her, "how do I try that Jesus?" She told me to ask JESUS into my heart. I asked her if I tried that Jesus for about three months would he work for me. She said to me to give it a try. I was going to try Jesus the way we try a witchdoctor, if he does not work we look for another powerful one. I made a decision that if He worked then I would keep going there for more help. I just wanted Jesus to solve my issues then I would go about my own business. So I accepted Jesus into my life. But put lots of conditions for him.

I was born again for a little while and for that time I was very sincere with the Lord. One of the girls gave me an old King James Version of the Bible and asked me to read it. When I read it I could not understand anything in it. I tried reading from Genesis to Revelation but nothing made sense to me. Each time I read the Bible I would fall asleep. I just read and read and did not understand a word. The spirit of Slumber or maybe the demons were stopping me from reading the Word of God.

During the first few months that I accepted Jesus into my life, life was a real struggle. During this period I could distinctly hear the voices of my relatives in Zimbabwe warning me that I was taking the wrong path. Remember they were not in England, we were oceans apart. Please read Acts 9:23-27. I had to renounce Jesus and go back to ancestral worship. They threatened to do evil to me and this made me so afraid that I was fearful of my life.

Creatures looking like bats started to come in my room and beat me making such a commotion there. This caused me to scream very loudly; people hearing it might think that I was having delusions. Here I was in my room screaming my head off. Bat like things were attacking me and I could not see them. A real classic case for a mental hospital! It was a real bad experience and I was alone. They flew around me really giving me a big fright. They would make such as noise that I would cover my head and hide under my bed because they were flying all over my head. I did not see these birds in the flesh but they used to make such ugly noises. When they left I was left with a lot of marks and bruises on my body. This made me so sure that I was not imagining these things. I was beginning to wonder if this is what being born again was about.

I did not have a solid foundation and I could not discuss what I was going through with anybody as I thought that they would think that I was crazy. The lady who led me to the Lord was moved to another place so I was basically on my own.

I decided to go back to what I was born into because coming to Jesus was giving me a lot of problems (2 Peter 2:22). "But it happened unto them according to the true proverb, the dog is turn to his own vomit again; and the sow that was washed to her wallowing in the mire." I resumed my former beliefs and practices. I left being born again and went back to what I knew. I did not actually renounce Jesus, but I did not follow his ways either. I mixed the ancestral worship and Jesus. I was so frightened of being on the wrong side of my people so I gave up. (Exodus 20:5, KJV) states that "Thou shalt not bow down thyself to them, nor serve them: for I the Lord thy God am a jealous God, visiting the iniquity of the fathers upon the children unto the third and fourth generation of them that hate me."

In my heart I wanted Jesus, but if I go to this Jesus did I get into so much trouble! I did not understand why life got so bad after the first time that I accepted Jesus into my life.

After I compromised my former beliefs with Christianity life became easier. The attacks stopped. I wanted Jesus but I dare not follow Him fully, as my life would be tormented. I could not grow in the Lord. I kept backsliding. In all I was born again about eight times in my life. It is only recently that I realised that I was born again for real. Each time I was born again. Again I would be sincere to the Lord for that period of time. Then the attacks would come and I would be so frightened backslide and so the cycle was endless. A real Catch 22 situation my life in the Lord was stagnant. There was no one to talk to, no one to confide in about the strange things that were happening in my life. I could see other people who were born again around me changing but as for me life was at a standstill. Only now do I understand why I could not grow in the Lord.

I did not have a proper foundation. I did not belong to a church. Again a curse was over my life. I was also demonically bound. I suggest that anyone who leads someone to the Lord be prepared to follow up with the person until the newly born again can understand the basics of salvation.

Unless that curse was broken and the demons in me cast out and I have proper teaching I would have NO SPIRITUAL GROWTH. To make matters worse, I did not even know that I was demonised or cursed.

When Jesus went about doing well on this earth, he preached the gospel, cast out devils, and healed the sick. (Mark 1:38 – 39) says that Jesus replied, "Let us go somewhere else to the nearby villages so I can preach there also, that is why I have come. So He travelled throughout Galilee preaching in their synagogues and driving out demons."

If I had the right foundation at the time of being born again, maybe if someone had discerned the spiritual condition that I was in, and cast out the devils that were in me at the time I received Jesus, I would have grown spiritually.

For this reason I sincerely believe that when one is born again, one has to be built upon a good foundation by the proper teachings and being thoroughly assessed spiritually by mature spirit filled born again elders, ministers or pastors. If they need deliverance then let the newly saved go through it. Also let these new converts have access to help and counselling to assist with their growth in the lord. Newly born again babies should be followed up and nurtured and taught the right foundation until they start to grow and understand the things of God. I believe that this is one of the reasons why the churches lose so many souls after they have been born again. YOU WOULD NOT LEAVE A NEW BORN BABY TO FEND FOR HIMSELF WOULD

YOU.WHAT IS THE DIFFERENCE WITH THE SPIRIT BABIES.
Jesus did not separate preaching, casting out devils or healing the sick.
(Matthew 9:35). States,

*"Jesus went through all the towns and villages, teaching in their synagogues, preaching the good news of the kingdom and healing every disease and sickness and casting out demons."*

The gospel is really being preached out there, most people have heard about Jesus but as in the parable of the Sewer in (Mark 4: 3 – 20), Jesus said,

*"Listen, a farmer went out to sow his seed: As he was scattering the seed, some fell along the path, and birds came and ate it up, some fell on rocky places, where it did not have much soil. It sprang up quickly, because the soil was shallow. But when the sun came up, the plants were scorched, and they withered because they had no root. Other seeds fell among thorns; which grew up and choked the plants so that they did not bear grain. Still other seed fell on good soil. It came up, grew and produced a crop multiplying thirty, sixty or even a hundred times. Then Jesus said, he who has ears let him hear."*

When Jesus was alone, his twelve disciples and the others around him asked him about the parables. He explained to them that "the secret of the Kingdom of God has been given to you. But to those on the outside everything is said in parables, so that they may be ever seeing but never perceiving, and ever hearing but never understanding, otherwise they might turn from their sins and be forgiven, then Jesus said to them don't you understand this parable? How then will you understand any parable? The farmer sows the word. Some people are like seed along the path where the word is sown. As soon as they hear it, Satan comes and takes away the word that was sown in them. Others are seed sown on rocky places, hear the word and receive it with joy. But since they have no root, they last only a short time. When trouble or persecution comes because of the word, they quickly fall away. Still others are like seed sown among thorns. They hear the word, but the worries of this life, the deceitfulness of wealth and the desires of other things to come in choke the word, making it unfruitful. Others are like seed sown on good soil hear the word, accept it and produce a crop thirty, sixty or even a hundred times when sown."

So that is what happened to me. Satan and his demons want to take as many people as he can to hell with him so he does everything he can to stop people from perceiving the good news of the gospel of Jesus Christ.

I used to go to church and get all excited but when I returned home, I forgot what the preacher had said. Sometimes I would feel so sleepy in the church and at times something would happen in the service that would distract me from hearing the word of God. My mind always wandered. I went to different churches and was not rooted in the Word.

# CHAPTER 8

## THE SPIRIT OF SINGLENESS

### THE SECOND MARRIAGE

There is a saying that time is a healer. So I got over the trauma of my first marriage. I had not gone to counselling or spoken to anyone about my plight. I had no wisdom to know that I had to first deal with the spirit of rejection and all the baggage that was affecting my life first. I had no idea that I had any demons in me. I did not know that the curse of singleness was operative in me. Lastly, I had no idea that I was married to a spiritual husband.

When I met my second husband, all was very good to begin with. I sincerely believed that he was the one for me. I had found the right man and we would grow old together. We agreed most of the time. Some few years into the marriage I began to have an urge to go to Zimbabwe. It felt like someone was calling my name and I had to go. I discussed this with my husband and we decided to go to Zimbabwe to see my relatives and take a holiday.

I went to introduce my husband to my aunt's relations. They were all at my granddad's house. When we got there we found them organising a traditional dance, in honour of my granddad. He had died the year before so at one year after death they are supposed to do this ceremony. This is done to invite the spirit of the dead back in the home to look after his family. The common belief in Africa is that if a person dies you have to invite the spirit back in the home after one year. They believe that the dead relatives are accommodating and friendly. They become our ancestors and they look after our welfare. They warn us of all the dangers that come from the spiritual realm. The dead ancestor will look after the family and will not let harm come to them. It is the duty of the family to organise this rite. It has to be done in a specific way. A lot of traditional beer is brewed. Some of the beer that was being brewed was to be taken to the grave of my granddad. This would be the special sacrifice to be able to call back the spirit to the family home. The people who came to the dance would drink the remaining beer. The other beer would be poured on the family altar as a libation.

Our relatives were very happy to see us. We sat and talked and caught up with a lot of family matters. They said things like it was very good that I came at that time because the ancestors called me. If you look into it properly we had the sudden urge to go to Zimbabwe. As soon as we got there it looked like they were waiting for us to be there. How did that happen? Now I know they can call you in the spirit and you will turn up in the physical. The ancestors knew that there would be a big family gathering in honour of the well-loved and well-respected grand dad.

While we were still talking among ourselves when there was a commotion outside. We got up to look. The masquerades had arrived. They were dancing violently. One of my aunts pushed us in my granddad's bedroom and locked us in there. We could see through the window the dancing of the masqueraders. They were naked except for the masks covering their faces. These are special ones that dance for the dead. They had sickles in their hands and the ladies were dancing provocative sexual dances with them. One of my aunts took a live chicken and gave it to them and they cut off its neck and poured the blood all over the yard. Some of the people were throwing money on them. Within a short time they collected a lot of money and chickens. As quickly as they had come they went away. My aunt was saying something like you always have to have a lot of chickens and money ready as they do not want to be kept waiting.

The killing of chicken or animals is blood sacrifice well known among the Africans. (Number 25:2-3). They use the spirit of the dead animal for evil. My aunts had live chickens ready for every single day of the ceremonial week until the end of the ceremony. The big dance with the many masquerades would be on the big night. Everybody would come and we would celebrate all night. At the end of the week they would all kill a goat. While they were killing the goat they had to speak special words to the ancestors on behalf of the whole family. The ones who were not present were presented too. The eldest is the first to peak then the one who follows after him and it goes on like that.

My ex-husband was so shaken he was so frightened as he had never seen or heard anything like this before. The reason this was done was to pay homage to the spirit of the dead. The masqueraders had to come to the house once daily. They danced around the house and performed their special rituals and killed an animal daily as a blood sacrifice. They would then pour the blood around the yard and continue to do whatever they were doing. This is supposed to please the dead. There cannot be mistakes or the absence of blood in these ceremonies. If a mistake is done or the blood sacrifice is not given or the ceremony is not done at all, there can be terrible consequences, for example, sudden death of a family member. Some horrible things will just start happening in the family like job losses, sickness, strife and other bad things. There is no mercy in the spirit realm!

Now I know that there is only one ultimate sacrifice. That is, Jesus the Son of the living God. He died once and for all. We do not need to be killing any animal to go to God when we need Jesus who accomplished the ultimate sacrifice. Jesus has prepared for us the way to the father. He is the only way to heaven. Any religion that demands blood is not of God, for only Satan demands blood!

SACRIFICING TO THE DEAD

Scripture says in (Deut 18:10 - 12):
> **10 Let no one be found among you my family who sacrifices his son or daughter in the fire, who practices divination or sorcery, interprets omens engages in witchcraft,**
> **11 or casts spells or who is a medium or spirits or who consults the dead.**

*12 Anyone who does these things is detestable to the Lord your God will drive out those nations before you. You must be blameless before the Lord your God.*

I was not blameless before the Lord and so was my family. We thought nothing of it. We believed we were doing the right thing. After the masquerades had left, my aunt advised me to visit the grave of my grandfather. This is done for everyone who is not present when there is a death in the family. The absentee had to go to the grave and have their presence noted. The family and the best friend of the family take the relative to the graveyard. I was very happy to oblige.

We went to the graveyard and when we arrived there the family friend advised us to kneel at the head of my granddad's grave. He said that we should pay lots of money to the dead. My ex husband did so and put lots of money on the grave. Then my aunt began to pray to the dead. She was asking the ancestors to look after us, to see us and to do good to us as we had come from far - we had come from England. She said a lot of things, which sounded good at the time. After the prayers, the family friend took the money and we returned to my grandparents' home.

When we got back we went to the bedroom where the family altar stood. Ever since I was a little girl I usually see my grandparents go to the altar a few times a week. This is situated at the top of my grand father's bed. On it is a special wooden plate. The plate always has some money in it. What they did was to get the elders of the family to kneel at the altar. They then make a respectful silence and pay homage to the ancestors. They do not go empty handed to the altar. They put some money and then speak to the family spirits. They say all their requests and problems and ask the ancestors to lead them and guide them.

On special occasions they brew traditional beer and pour some on the altar and go around the yard pouring beer and speaking to the family spirits all the time. Usually the elder of the family always does that. That elder is the high priest of the family altar. These individuals have enormous demonic power. They rule the family with an iron fist. If you ever cross their paths these priests or priestesses make your family life hell. They deal with all the spiritual problems in the family. They have ways of knowing whatever you do or wherever you are. Most families in Africa have altars in their homes. The priesthood is passed on from generation to generation.

The following weekend we had a big traditional dance at my mother's house. This was to unveil the tombstone on my father's grave. I had to do all this as I was there for only a short time. I had to do all these rituals so that all would go well with me. Many people came and we danced all night. Early in the morning we all made a procession to go to the graveyard.

My brother advised me to change lots of money. He wanted me to be throwing it all along on the way to my father's grave. I was happy to do so. At the graveside the traditional rituals were done. The Christians also offered their prayers. This is what was expected of me. I was so proud to have done my part as a dutiful daughter.

Scripturally, I was very wrong to participate in this.

For (Leviticus 19:31) says,
> **"Do not turn to mediums or seek out spiritist for they will defile you. I am the Lord your God."**

Now let me speak realistically and practically to someone reading this book. When a person dies what happens to them? When we bury the dead person what happens to the body? What happens to the spirit of the dead person? As born again people we know that if you die in Christ you go to heaven. If you are not in Christ you go to hell. We bury the body in the grave, your spirit does not die but it goes to heaven or hell.

So we know that if you are dead the body is left in the ground but the spirit does not die. It either goes to heaven or to hell depending on where you stood with the Lord Jesus (Luke 16: 19-31).

- 65 -

In Africa as I have already noted, most cultures worship the dead. They perform special rituals to appease the spirit of the dead. They treat the dead better that they treat the living. They do everything in their power to fulfil the rituals of the dead. A person can be very sick for a long time. No one will give him a little money or medicine. As soon as he dies they will do everything to give him a decent burial. They will even borrow money to bury the dead and perform the expected rituals for the dead. The people dress in a special way and do special rituals. Children do special rituals to prove that they are real children of the deceased. Wives engage in special ceremonies to please the dead husbands.

One of my uncles died a few years ago and his body was lying in the bedroom before the burial. One of my aunts asked if my cousin's little daughter could go into the bedroom alone and converse with her uncle and pick up something that was in the bedroom. The little girl's mother prevented her daughter from doing this. The aunt then asked another cousin's little girl to do that and the mother of the little girl agreed to it. Up to now we do not know exactly what happened in the bedroom between the corpse and that little girl. But what we do know for a fact is that after a week the little girl died. She was an innocent victim of worshipping the spirit of the dead.

I have good friends that come from Ghana and they tell me that their funerals cost more than the weddings. I know of some people who borrow tens of thousands from the bank just to go and bury their dead in a particular way.

I have observed this with a lot of Christians. They have a memorial for the dead. I have searched the scriptures and found nothing that states that you should have a memorial for the dead. As children of light, we are allowed to mourn but we mourn with a purpose. When we grieve with no understanding we open up our spirit to demons. As a result I have seen a lot of people who come from funerals with a lot of problems. I encourage anyone who loses someone to mourn but do this with hope and understanding that the dead are either in heaven or in hell.

I have counselled a lot of people who say that they dream of the dead. These could be relations, friends etc. They usually have one thing in common after they dream of the dead. Their life starts going wrong. Things start falling apart.

Once I dreamt of my dead father whom I loved very much. I dreamt that he was trying to marry me to a man and was giving me permission to marry that man. When I woke up I was so disturbed by that dream. In that month a lot of bad things just happened to me. I also used to have this recurrent dream that I was arranging my own funeral and I would be eating and drinking in the dream. After these bad dreams I would be very ill and things would not go well for me.

Now I am born again and anointed by Jesus I now know how to take authority over any spirit that is not of the Lord Jesus in the name of Jesus. I now know how to pray and cancel every evil programme of the enemy in the name of Jesus. When you dream things from the dead people it not good to go for advice from the people who consult the spirit of the dead.

(Leviticus 20:6) says that if you go for advice from the people who consult the spirit of the dead God will reject you and set His face against you, and cut you from among His people. This lets me know that I should not mix my Jesus with wizards and familiar spirits and any such things or people.

From the examples I have given you, you can now understand why some of the things that happened to me have happened in that fashion.


THE SECOND DIVORCE

On our return to England we started to have lots of trouble in our marriage. We started to fight like cat and dog. I would often lose my temper and would throw tantrums. My husband would be so nasty to me and sometimes physically abuse me. Twice I left him and twice I returned. I was always sick and had two surgical procedures done Money was dwindling away and we could not see what we were doing with our money. We were paid very well but we were not moving forward. Things were not right and we could not figure out why it was like that.

We had no idea with the ways of God. If you can recall in the earlier chapters we talked about losing money. Money just seemed to disappear from us. I could not figure out what was happening in my life. I knew something was wrong - something had gone wrong, but I did not know how to fix it. I started to party seriously but that brought no joy to my life. I would go out clubbing to all the fun functions around London, but still no joy.

When a marriage is not working a woman will know that things are not working. When things that used to be right go wrong and you start seeing the same pattern of things happening you will know the signs. I had no power to correct them. The alarms bells will start ringing!

I started going to a small church in Bed font. Even though I was going to church I was still going to carnival, dance halls and all the things that a real born again should not do. I used to drink, quarrel and had a very bad temper. There was no pastor in the church. So I did not get proper pastoral care. The church was full of elderly people. They were lovely and committed to God. The more I went to that church the worse my life at home became. I began to smell sulphurous smells around me. These smells terrorised me. Each time I smelt the bad smell I knew that there would be trouble at my home.

I worked with a good Christian woman whom I would beg to pray for me. I did not explain to her that I was afraid to go home because I knew we would have a big row as soon as I got home. Anything would trigger the rows. It was torture. She would faithfully pray with me each time that I asked her to pray for me. I told her that I was also a Christian. She began to question my walk with the Lord, as she was not happy with the state I was in. She told me that something was not right in me but she did not know what it was. I told her about what was happening in my home. I did not mention the ancestral rituals we used to do in Africa. She stood with me in prayer.

I also began to read the Bible again but I still read it like a novel. I would just read and read but I had no understanding at all. One-day things were so bad at home that I just cried out to God. I lifted the Bible up to God and cried "God who is mentioned in this Bible if you are real and alive please kill me today or get me out of this bad marriage". I soon forgot that prayer but God did not forget. Within forty-eight hours of praying that prayer God had me out of that marriage. He did not kill me. Thank God!

Here is how it happened. I was studying anaesthetics at Thames Valley University. I had an assignment to submit. I needed to meet the deadline so I was working very hard between work at home and University. I stayed in work to type up my assignment and finish it. By the time I finished all it was 2am. When I got home everyone was asleep. I also went to sleep. Then the ex-husband woke up and was towering over me. He was asking me about where I was, and I told him that I was studying and had to finish off my assignment. He knew that, but for some reason he did not believe me. He was accusing me of every other thing but the study. It was not the first time for me getting home late, however, that day I was later than usual and he was really mad at me. He kicked me out of bed. When I looked at him, his eyes were red - a colour that was not his own.     I realised that I was not talking to a person that was in his normal senses but to something else. Something had definitely possessed him

He was threatening to go downstairs to get a knife and stab me. I knew he meant it. So when he went to get the knife downstairs I did not wait to be stabbed, I jumped out of the window and ran for my life. I was only wearing a nightgown in the October cold. I managed to call the police from a nearby phone box. Then I went to hide under the cars. When he realised that I was missing he went to my daughter's bedroom, woke her up and kicked her. He beat her up really bad.

My friend Alice was visiting from Zimbabwe heard the commotion, so she woke up to find him beating up my daughter. She intervened and then he stopped. I always thank my friend Alice for saving my daughter's life. Maybe if my friend had not been there, my daughter could have been killed. He took my friend in the car and was going up and down the streets looking for me. I was hiding and I only came out when the police arrived. He came up to the police car and he was ranting and raving so much that the police decided it was not safe for me to go back to the house with him.

The police took us back to the house to collect some overnight clothes. I left like a dog with my clothes in a black bag. The police took me to a friend's house. While I waited on the next instruction the police gave me a strong warning about going back to him. They saw how out of control he was and said I can only go back at my own risk. I was so traumatised by what had happened. It happened again, same pattern. One minute I am in a marriage the next minute I'm not. The same cycle continued repeating itself and I began to wonder what was wrong with me.

Even if I wanted to or tried very hard to keep the marriage something had to happen. Something had gone wrong again and it was beyond my control. That something was unpredictable and I was always caught unaware. I was doing it in my own strength and the curse that was in my life was not dealt with. There was no way I could keep the marriage in my own strength. Still I had no idea that there was a spirit in my life and that the spirits were causing all the bad things that were happening in my life to happen.

I was so cut up by the break up of my marriage. I knew something was wrong in my life but I could not put a finger on it. I wanted to find out what was wrong with me but I was far from the witchdoctors and mediums that I used to consult. I was so sad and depressed that I went to see my doctor because I could not sleep at night. My general practitioner referred me to a psychiatrist who was not of much help; I was not mad, just sad! My problem was one of the heart and spiritual. No psychiatrist or medical person could help me

I am a nurse myself so I have the greatest respect for the medical and nursing profession. The psychiatrist said that nothing was wrong with me. I was so sick and the doctors could not pin point what was wrong with me but I was very sickly.

## THE DEMONIC TORMENT

After I moved in with a friend I began to smell even more dipterous smells around me. Now I realize that demons smell bad. Unnatural fear engulfed me. Each time I smelt these smells I would know that something bad was around me. I knew that something bad was going to happen. I would be paralysed with fear. I could fear even my own shadow. If I thought I saw my ex's car or what I thought looked like his car I would freeze like a rabbit caught by some sudden light. I would shake like a leaf. They call these symptoms "panic attacks". I started to have bad dreams and nightmares. It started with men having sex with me in the dream. They would rape me violently and there was nothing I could do about it. I felt very dirty and useless. In the dream it would be like somebody was force-feeding me. I could not avoid these dreams. I only woke up after the damage was done. I also drank red drinks in my dream. I would find myself in terrible situations in the dream. I was seeing snakes, vicious dogs and allsorts of wild animals in my dreams.

When I woke up from these dreams I would be sicker and more confused. I kept on reading my Bible and praying. In spite of this these things did not go away. Because I did not know how to pray I could only repeat the Lord's Prayer over and over.

I would also pray Solomon's prayer of Dedicating the Temple. (2Chr:12-42) or the Believer's Prayer in (Acts 4:23 – 31).

My dreams seemed so real and it affected me adversely.

# SEX IN THE DREAM

When I was having sex in the dream I used to enjoy it if it was not violent. I did not know that it was a bad thing to be having sex in the dream with an unknown being. Joshua my husband was telling me that he was telling one of his friends that having sex in the dream was not good, but he laughed him to scorn because he thought it was good Joshua knew that he was having trouble with the law. He was also banned from his marital home and he had to stay at his mother's. We believe that it was a spirit wife that was having sex with him. This demon causes singleness, confusion and strife in marriages Joshua was asking him to renounce those dreams and repent. But he did not take his advice for he regarded it for a joke. Not long afterwards he was sent to prison for sexual assault. He is now on deportation order. May the Lord have mercy upon him?

(Job 33:14-24) says:

> For God speaketh once, yea twice, yet man perceiveth it not. In a dream, in a vision for the night, when deep sleep falleth upon men, in slumbering upon the bed; Then he openeth the ears of man, and sealeth the ears of men, and seals their instruction. That he may withdraw man from his purpose, and hide pride from man. He keepeth back his soul from the pit, and his life from perishing by the sword. He is chastened also with pain upon his bed, and the multitude of his bones with pain: So that his life abhorrent bread, and his soul dainty meat. His flesh is consumed away, that it cannot be seen; and his bones that were not seen stick out. yeas his soul draweth near unto the grave and his life to the destroyers. If their be a messenger with him an interpreters, one among a thousand, to show unto man his uprightness;
> 24 then he is gracious unto him, and said, deliver him from going down to the pit: I have found a ransom

Please read (Job 33:25 -30). I had no idea that it was a spirit. I did not know that the things that were happening in my dream were real in the spirit realm. They would affect me in the physical realm. I only realised it after a teaching sermon on spiritual warfare was taught in one of the services that I got knowledge and understanding. I would advise anybody who has sex in the dream to know that it is very demonic in nature. I encourage you to seek deliverance from that spirit as soon as possible.

The purpose of the spirit wife or husband is to destroy your life especially married life. You can either marry but your marriage will not last. You keep divorcing or losing your partner by death or any painful way. Sometimes you can want to get married but you only meet partners who waste your time, when it comes to real commitment they run and marry someone else. Maybe you really want to marry but nobody looks at you for marriage. Other people might hate commitments so much that they only want to have relationships with people who are married already. You can also be so hard hearted for example you want physical relationships with the opposite sex but you don't want to get married.

Some people say "I just want a boyfriend or a girlfriend". The Word of God is very clear to get married is "good", not to get married is also "good".

It is advisable that if you know that you will not burn with lust and you do not want to marry then that is ok. But if you know that you burn with lust it is advisable to get married. If you have sex outside of marriage a curse will befall you. Please do not let yourself be used as a sex object. Not when you know the laws of God. In the dream the sex is real. The purpose for the sex in the dream is that the agent of darkness will use it for your own destruction usually for that to happen the demons have a legal right to violate you.

In my culture it is an open secret that if a murder is committed, a young virgin is usually sent to live and be married in the family of the murdered person. This is to repay for evil deed done and so that a curse will not befall that person. In these modern times the young ladies refuse to do that. But what usually happens is the elders of the family can dedicate the girl without her knowledge and the girl will never know.  She might find out when she comes to Jesus or when she goes to the witchdoctors.

These spirits are very jealous and they can harm and confuse your partner.  Please note that if you are always angry with your partner for no apparent reason or violent towards your partner or vow never to get married (unless it is the will of God for you) but you like sex before marriage, then a spiritual wife or husband could be operating in your life. It causes the spirit of lust.

Some people use astral projections to enter into the bedrooms of their victims and this lust them sexually. This is curse of using witchcraft. My very good friend was telling me that there was a big row at her husband's place of work. The boss sacked one worker. When he was leaving he said to the boss, "You have a very nice bedroom" and was describing the boss's bedroom to him. The boss asked him how he knew that the sacked worker said "remember that your wife was complaining about a spirit that comes to sleep with her and the entire nocturnal visitation. It was the worker who did it to spite him".

My best friend is married to a policeman. He came home in shock one day and was describing what had happened on his shift to his wife. He said that they were investigating a crime scene so they went to wake up the occupants of one house. In the house an old lady was in bed with a young man, and the police thought it unusual. They asked the old lady who that man was and she said that it was her son. The young man was not aware of what was happening. He was in a deep sleep. The mum was using her son for sex. What an abomination!

In one of the revival meetings in Kenya, a man who was mentally ill was set free from his mental disorder. He came to give his testimony. He said that since he was a little boy his grandmother used him for sex. We were so amazed at this. A lot of rape happens in the sleep. The damage is still done.

Here in England it was in the newspapers that some famous Hollywood stars had spiritual sex. The media was talking about it like it was a good thing. It is not; it results in spiritual bondage. I will explain in detail in

# CHAPTER 9

## DEMONIC ODOURS

I used to smell sulphurous odours smelling like sulphur. At this particular time it was exaggerated. I had no idea why the smell was so bad. The smell used to make me so afraid. I would start shaking like a leaf and at times I could hardly drive. My body would freeze. Sometimes I would faint with fear. I had no idea where the fear was coming from. I did not know what the smell was. It got so bad that I started to entertain suicidal thoughts many times. It was as if somebody was urging me to do it but I never saw the person urging me to do it I just heard them. Now I am aware that demons can encourage you to kill yourself. They also smell and I smelt them quite often. For this reason I discourage believers from going into in shops where they burn incense. What are they trying to hide in there?

I believe most of them are trying to hide the stench of the demons. (Read Rebecca Brown's book "He came to set the captives free", chapter 4 page 43).

I was recently listening to the tapes by Mary K Baxter on the revelation of hell. She said in her testimony that hell stinks. The demons smell very bad and they have an unnatural odour. When I was ministering in a certain church in Canada I happened to mention this. A lady came up to me at the end of the service. She said to me that her daughter used to smell a repugnant odour about her. We ministered to her but we have not heard any feed back from her. We believe that God was able to set her daughter free, as the mum stood in proxy for her.

These things are real and they are happening to a lot of people. My very good friend said to me that when she was going through her deliverance she always experienced bad smells around her and that no perfume or air freshener could stop that smell. After her deliverance these bad odours disappeared.

## EATING AND DRINKING IN THE DREAM

In my dream I saw myself eating and also drinking red drinks. The witches would feed me anything they liked in the dream as I had no power to resist. In the morning when I woke up my belly will be swollen and very sore. I would be belching and passing bad wind. I used to feel so ashamed about these bad habits. I had no control over it. I tried most of the medicines to relieve it but it did not help me. I used to wake up with bad tummy aches. It felt like somebody was cutting up my intestines and I would pass blood through my rectum.

Doctors diagnosed Crohn's disease but I later discovered that it was witchcraft. It is also common knowledge in Africa that witches and Satanist eat human flesh. When you come across the witches accusing each other of whatever they did to each other they talk like this "you said we should eat my child first then we would eat yours next. Why did you start with mine? Or "You killed the wrong one." The witches go to the graveyards to eat the dead. From what I know they cannot enter the graves of true men and women of God (2 King 6:24-30).

I now pray and cover the graves of all my relations with the blood of Jesus. David speaks about this in (Psalms 14 verse 4, King James Version).

Have all the workers of iniquity no knowledge? Who eat up my people as they eat bread, and they call not upon the Lord.

The spirit of death and destruction was very strong in me. I was in error to think that death would relieve my suffering. I did not know that if I committed suicide I would go straight to hell. That is a bad place to go, as there is no chance to repent.

## NIGHTMARES

At times I would dream that I was fighting in my dream. I would find myself wandering in an evil forest. I would be seeing myself chased by evil animals. I would see snakes in the dream. When I woke in the mornings I would be so physically tired like I was in a real fight. Also were ever these animals had had contact with me in the dream I would wake up with a painful mark on that part .At times sleep would just elude me all night, then in the early hours of the morning I would start dozing. When I doze I would then feel these hands choking me, or a big body sitting on me. I would not even cry out for help my voice would fail me. I could try so much to wake up but it felt like I was paralysed. I lost a lot of weight, and I looked like a skeleton. The other common dream was when I saw myself jumping off tall buildings or falling into a bottomless hole and I would be screaming in my sleep.

I say to parents to be alert to what their children say to them. Children are very sensitive in the spirit. If your child is having nightmares, please do not ignore them and say they are just nightmares, and they will go away. Anoint your children and cover them with the blood of Jesus. What they see is really happening in the spirit realm. Teach your children spiritual warfare too. God honours the prayers of children. Their angel is always standing before his throne.


## MASQUERADERS

Because I was involved in these from the time I was born I would dream about them all the time. The most vivid dream is when they would be trying to be nice to me in the dream. They would offer me all the good things I used to have before. Remember by the this time I had lost everything I owned I had lost my house my good job my car and my health . Also each time these masquerades came to me in the dream they offered me snuff in my sleep. They often succeeded in doing what ever they came to do to me in the dream. I had no power or knowledge how to resist these attacks. These attacks went on for a long time.

A lot of people see the carnival as a harmless thing. If you notice they wear different masks. Each mask represents a demon god. So they will be giving honour to demon gods. I would only go to the carnival if the Lord tells me to go and evangelise. Going to the carnival is participating in the demon worship.


## DEAD RELATIVES/ FRIENDS NEIGHBOURS

I use to dream of dead relatives and ancestors. I used to think that it was good to dream of the dead as I was taught that the dead are our ancestors. Before I was born again the dead people whom I saw in the dream used to give me advice and I would wake up feeling very happy If I followed their advice and things went well with me for that time only. If I did not do what they said things got very ugly. In my culture we are encouraged to say out the dreams of when the dead come. It is seen as a good omen according to the culture. But the laws of God are different we do not mix with the dead. As you know that the dead are either in heaven or in hell these dreams are very bad. The demons assume the faces of the dead people especially the ones you like a lot or the ones you loved and masquerade as them. Usually the demons like to take the faces of the grandmother, grandfather, mother or father. The ones we usually respect the most or the ones we usually fear them the most. The whole idea is to curse you and bring confusion in your life.

It is the art of necromancy sometimes during these times another person can be invoking the spirit of the dead to manipulate the destiny of the dreamer and or lead them to participate in witchcraft and superstition. Satan tries to make things look nice and harmless but we now know that he is the master of deception and he presents himself as an angel of light.

# DEMONIC ALTARS

(Judges 6:11) reads:

> "The angel of the Lord came and sat down under the oak tree in Ophrah that belonged to Joash the Abiezarite, where his son Gideon was threading wheat at the wine press to keep it from the Midianites."

(Judges 6:12 – 27) says:

*When the angel of the Lord appeared to Gideon he said, the Lord is with you mighty warrior.*

*But Sir Gideon replied if the Lord is with us why has all this happened to us Where are all the wonders that our fathers told us about when they said, did he not bring us up out of the land of Egypt. But now the Lord has abandoned us into the land of the Midianites.*

*The Lord turned to him and said go in the strength you have and save Israel out of the Midianites' hands. Am I not sending you?*

*But Lord how can I save Israel my clan is the weakest and I am the least in my family.*

*The Lord answered I will be with you, and you will strike down all the Midianites together.*

*Gideon replied if I have found favour in your eyes give me a sign that it is really you talking to me.*

*Please do not go away until I come back and bring my offering and set it before you. And the Lord said I will wait until you return.*

*Gideon wet and prepared a young goat, and from an ephah of flour he made bread without yeast. Putting the meat in the basket and its broth in the pot he brought them out and offered them to him under the oak tree.*

*The angel of God said to him, take the meat and the unleavened bread, place them on this rock and pour out the broth. And Gideon did so.*

*With the tip of his staff that was in his hand the angel of the Lord touched the meat and the unleavened bread. Fire flared from the rock, consuming the meat and the bread. And the angel of the Lord disappeared.*

*When Gideon realised that it was the angel of the Lord, he exclaimed ah sovereign lord I have seen the angel of the Lord face to face.*

*But the Lord said unto him, peaces do not be afraid. You are not going to die.*

*So Gideon built an altar there and called it the Lord is peace. To this day it stands in Ophrah of the Abiezarite.*

*That same night the lord said to him take the second bull from your father's herd, the one seven years old.*

*Tear down your fathers alter to Baal and cut down the Asherah pole beside it. Then build a proper kind of altar to the Lord your God on top of this height. Using the wood of the Asherah pole that you cut down, offer a second bull as a burnt offering.*

*So Gideon took ten of his servants and did as the Lord told him. But because he was afraid of his family he and the men of the town, he did it at night rather than in the daytime. In the morning when the men of the town got up there was Baal's alter demolished with the Asherah pole beside it cut down and the second bull sacrificed on the newly built altars.*

If you read on you will see the anger that Gideon's action brought to the family and the town.

Now I will try to explain to you why I gave the example of Gideon and his fathers alters. In Judges Chapter 11, verse 11), when the angel of the Lord approached Gideon and gave him a powerful greeting he could not take it. Instead of finding out why the Angel was greeting him like that he started complaining. He had nothing positive to say about himself or his tribe.

Secondly here was a true Israelite. He knew about God and what God had done for his forefathers. I believe that he knew about the laws of God and yet in his father's house there was an altar of Baal. He could only complain to God but he did not remember to confess his sins or why the Israelites got to be in the circumstances, which they were in.

- 82 -

According to (Judges 11:14) How could he expect a breakthrough in his life while he lived in a polluted house with altars to other gods the altar of Baal was pure idolatry and witchcraft God hates that. He is a jealous God and we should have no other gods besides the God in heaven. In verse 14, he got a positive send off from the Angel of the Lord. The angel of the Lord affirmed who he was in God. So he was strengthened in the Lord. He gets lots of reassurance from the angel of the Lord. If God says he is with you he really means he will smite your enemies.

In (verse 18) he understood the principle of offering to God. In the first offering God accepted that offering by his grace. When he saw the offering being consumed, Gideon perceived that he had seen the angel of the Lord. Thank God he did not die. He called the altar peace. SHALLOM, SHALLOM, SHALLOM!!

In verse 25: This is my point. God said to Gideon, "Before you Gideon go any further I want you to get rid of the altars of Baal that your father has.

Before I go to war with you get rid of your Baal altars. Before I deliver you, you need to get rid of the Baal and his altars. Before we do any Godly business I want you Gideon to get rid of Baal altar. Before you offer me a second offering, let us deal with your father's demonic altars.

Now it is difficult when a child is born again and the parents are into idol worship or any other thing that does not glorify God. The altars that their father has affect their walk with God. These need to be demolished totally.

While there was Baal worship in the house of the Gideon's father, Gideon and Israel were oppressed. He was in poverty. He lived in fear. He was a slave. He could only talk about what God did many years ago but he did not experience it until after he got rid of Baal altars in his father's house.

Now in the case of Gideon, you may say that he lived many years ago.

He is dead now how does that affect us? But no, it certainly does affect us today. Let me ask you one question, who is your father?

Who is your dad? Who does your dad worship?
Are you born again and do you truly know Jesus?
You can quote scriptures, go to church and do all the right things but life remains an uphill task. For you to get anything worthwhile it is a struggle, while other people get things easy.

I mentioned in the above chapters how most homes and villages in Africa have altars. I mentioned about special rituals for the dead, for birth of children, marriages, travelling, sin offerings and others. So again just these questions to you: Who is your father? What is in his house? Whom does he worship? Who is the priest or priestess serving at the altar of your family what are they saying about you? Is it positive or is it negative? What are they doing with your spiritual life? Where do you come from?

I want you to stop reading for a little while and start thinking of you and the family where you come from.    Think of what they do.

Some families do thing very secretly. They would still call your name to the gods of the family even though you do not agree with them anymore. You need the Holy Spirit to reveal all the demonic things that may be happening in your life. When you know you are dealing with them, remember we have the Holy Spirit to protect us. We have Jesus. Even if you have no idea just pray anyway. We have our Jehovah what is more with your spiritual welfare.

SOLUTION

We must allow the Holy Spirit to destroy all the spiritual altars in our lives. If you can destroy the physical altars do so as some things need to come down like what Gideon did. The altars need to be scattered and destroyed. The blood of Jesus is powerful enough to destroy all the works of Satan. It is important to repent of the sins of your grandparents done on their altars. Jesus is able to set you free! The Holy Spirit also sends fire to the evil priest and priestess who sacrifice at the altar.

If they do not repent they will be destroyed. When you do that the family or the whole village get upset. The witchdoctors will get very annoyed because by your warfare in the spirit you are upsetting their livelihood. I have had incidences when the elders make a phone call to the person praying begging the one praying to stop as the priest or priestess would be dying.

The day I found out about these demonic altars in my life, I prayed and I was set free from these evil forces. The altars of witchcraft, Obeah, black Magic, juju, n anga and whatever is not of God. When I finished denouncing and repenting of those things I felt so free. When I went to bed on the same night I had a vision of someone that was burnt as if someone had poured acid on him. They were imploring me to have mercy on them and to stop praying like I do.

WE CAN ONLY WIN THE BATTLE IN THE LORD WHEN WE GET RID OF ALL THE ALTARS IN OUR LIVES AND OR IN YOUR FATHER'S LIFE. WE HAVE A GOD WHO DOES NOT FAIL. HE IS FAITHFUL FOREVERMORE.

When you read the entire story of Gideon we see how God delivered the entire body of Israel with only three hundred men.

> (II Chronicles 14:11) reads *"Then Asa called to the Lord and said, Lord there is no one like you to help the powerless against the mighty. Help us, O Lord our God, for we rely in your name, we have come against this vast army. O Lord you are our God, do not let man prevail against you."*

GOD IS ABLE TO WIN YOUR BATTLE FOR YOU.

## ALTARS ON THE BODIES OF NORMAL HUMAN BEINGS:

Some people have demonic altars within them. Here is an example. Some men or women love themselves too much. They love themselves more than they love God or anything in this world. Others idolise their homes or their children's husbands or other thing before God. They love the things of this world. The god of other people is money, fame and whatever they put their hearts before GOD JEHOVAH.

Some men boast that they can have any charm any woman they like. They use special powers to manipulate women for sex.

Others use their body as an altar. They have special powers in their mouth when they speak ill about you evil things happens to you.
Some have evil power in their eyes. When they look at you with that evil eye, they destroy your life or destiny with that evil look.

Others use their hands for evil to destroy the work of innocent people.

Some use their private parts to confuse people and destroy them by sexual intercourse The men are totally ruined only because sex with these women Some men are addicted to pornographic websites or magazines. What are the women posing these magazines there doing to them? Some look on nakedness as harmless fun. This is no harmless fun. It has consequencies

In the summer some women dress to destroy men. They expose their legs and various parts of their anatomy. Men driving by looking as they can fall prey to this and can be disconnected. This can cause a lot of car accidents.

Some men and women are agents of Satan who have been sent to destroy the pastors and the church. I was discussing these demonic altars on the bodies with my husband today the 12<sup>th</sup>,of May 2006.

Lo and behold when I went to my church on the same evening, my archbishop was talking about a woman who came to seek counsel from him that very afternoon. He said and I quote. "Today I met Satan." That statement in itself got my full attention. He said Satan did not come to him in the physical sense but in the form of a woman who was the agent of Satan and who came to confess all the things she was trying to do to him and to our ministry. The ministry I attend is a very powerful and anointed ministry. We follow the ways of Jesus totally.

WE SEE JESUS EVERYDAY. POEPLE ARE SET FREE IN THE NAME OF JESUS. DEMONS ARE CAST OUT IN THE NAME OF JESUS. WE SEE JESUS HEAL THE SICK ALL THE TIME.

We have a powerful praying ministry. We also get many Satanic attacks.

The archbishop said that a woman came to confess to him and that she was no ordinary woman. She was an agent of Satan. She said that from the age of three she was such a horrible child that the whole village in Africa where she comes from knew that she was evil. Apparently she does not know how she became a witch but all she knows is that she has always been a witch since her childhood days. She knew that she was going to hell and she did not care.

She said that she used to have top-level meetings with Satan and he used to tell her what to do, whom to destroy and such things. Her mission was to take as many people as possible to hell with her. She said that she had killed many people by her evil powers. She also was responsible for giving nasty diseases to the people who crossed her path. She was able to afflict them with cancer, HIV, fibroids or any disease you could think about. She has made many people suffer became of her evil ways.

When she was in school she was the head girl of her school. She made sure that she used her position properly. She used to initiate all the girls in the school to be into witchcraft. This was done with or without their permission. She would take them to the river at certain hours of the night. She had the powers to manipulate them. She would do her satanic rituals and dances until the spirit of Satan possessed the girls. They in turn would become witches. Afterwards they initiated others.

She also drank blood. What I would like to know is whose blood she drank. How did she get it? What was the reason for drinking it? She also had evil power emanating from her eyes - she would either kill her enemies by one wicked look. She admitted that she had slept with countless number of men. How many she doesn't know. Every man that she has slept with has been destroyed or died within three months. Destruction and death followed every one with whom she slept.

From her country it is very hard to get a visa to travel to Europe. She to Europe by the power of Satan One day she decided to travel to Europe. She obtained her visa the next day. Satan helped her to get her visa with ease. She had it in mind to work as a prostitute in one of the European countries.

Please read (Proverbs Chapter7).

When she arrived at the Airport she was travelling with an African passport but she was allowed to pass through where the European passport holders passed through. She said as soon as she did she saw the officer who was checking the entrees into the country. She put a spirit of lust into him. The officer was so confused that he followed her to the baggage area and he pushed the trolley for her. He asked her for her telephone number. She told him that she had nowhere to stay and had just arrived in the country for the first time. He paid the hotel bill for her, had sex with her and returned to his wife. The following day his wife was involved with a traffic accident and she died.

Instead of mourning for his wife the officer went chasing after her and asked her to marry him. She refused. She said she took money from men by her charm. Men would give her all their money and savings they had. She manipulated so many men and they all gave her the money they had worked hard for and they died mysteriously. She then went to work in a brothel.

Apparently in some European countries prostitution is legal. She had taken on loans in order to go to Europe so she needed to work hard as a prostitute to be able to pay back these loans. In order to repay these loans it was necessary for her to sleep with at least fifteen men per day.

On her first day on the job she was not sleeping with as many men as she was supposed to she only managed to sleep with three. The minimum was supposed to be fifteen. The Madame of the brothel was not pleased with her performance. She confronted her and told her that she was not pleased with her performance. She verbally abused her. In response to the verbal attack she told the Madame that she would be dead in three days. The Madame then gave her a sound thrashing. True to her word after three days the Madamme of the brothel died of an apparent she had heart attack.

The people who had heard the row reported her to the police. For that reason she fled that country and ended up in the United Kingdom.

In the United Kingdom she continued her evil ways. Her mission was to destroy pastors and churches. She used to have sex with the pastors. She said the pastors had to sleep with her whether they liked it or not. She had special power to mesmerize the pastors. By the time they realised what has happened to them she would have done the damage already. After that the pastors' lives would be ruined. And their churches closed. She would sleep with at least three men per day.

How was she able to attract them? She would frequent nightclubs and all those places that are open at night. Her latest mission was to come and destroy our church. She was appointed by Satan to destroy our church. She admitted that she tried to seduce the archbishop since 2004. Each time she tried to do so she would see a hedge of fire around him. That would frighten her. She tried all her tricks on him and all her powers did not work. This bishop is one man I call a true servant of God. He teaches us by example to walk in the ways of Christ. He is entirely dedicated to serving Christ. He is a stickler for holiness.

She said that when there was an attack on our church Satan and his agents were responsible for it. She encouraged many of our members to leave the church. There was a time when we as a church went through much persecution and we lost many of our church members. That woman was encouraging members to leave the church. The strong of heart and the faithful stayed until the storm had blown over. Even still all her attempts to ruin the church failed.

The last time she attempted to do something evil the Lord Jesus himself appeared to her and he told her in no uncertain terms that if she tried one more time to destroy His servant, the Man of God, our beloved archbishop of our church and his members she would be destroyed totally. She was told to go and confess to him if she did not she would surely die. This caused her to panic. Her mission has failed. She was in trouble with Satan and the top satanic council. In the Satan's kingdom if you do not achieve your mission punishment is meted out to you. Sometimes even causing death,

She was so afraid of dying that she tried to find refuge in the very one who she was trying to destroy. God has a sense of humour.

In all these years the archbishop was not aware of what she was trying to do. It was just like the case with Balaam and Balak. The children of Israel had no idea someone was up to no good. They were eating, sleeping and getting on with life as usual. God was taking care of the enemy. My archbishop is a man of strong faith. He believes that if you harm him, his family or the members of his church our God will give you your reward. I know that this is true.

Satan does not fight fair. The battle with Satan is real. Do not be fooled. The war exists and the casualties are real. Do not perish because of ignorance. Check your life and see what is going right in your life or what is going wrong. Is it spiritual and it is physical? In this case the woman was advised to go to deliverance session for quite some time.

She needed to be rooted in the Lord. She had to truly renounce all her evil ways with the satanic kingdom. She also has to put a lot of effort for her to be delivered and walk with the Lord. Please read (Exodus Chapter 32) if you want to look at what happened with Aaron and the Israelites when Moses went up mount Sinai. They went crazy and were committing every abomination under the sun.

MISCELLANEOUS THINGS THAT COULD LEAD TO DEMONIC INTERFERENCE

Please note there are many ways that can lead to demons entering a person. These are some of the things I know that can open a doorway for demons to enter a person:

Cursing or mistreating the Jews - deceiving knowingly, being adulterous, if you disobey the Lord's commandments, - keeping or owning cursed objects. - When you refuse to come to the help of the Lord, when your house is wicked, when you refuse to give to the poor. Thieves and those who swear falsely by the name of the Lord, ministers of the Word of God who fail to give the glory to God. Robbing God of tithes and offerings, men who hearken to their wives rather than God, - when you dishonour your parents.

Creating graven images wilfully cheating people out of their properties taking advantage of blind people, oppressing strangers, widows, or the fatherless when you sleep with your father's wife Lying with any beast, if you commit incest When you smite your neighbour secretly Pride, trusting in men instead of the Lord, doing the work of the Lord deceitfully rewarding evil for good Having illegitimate children, for ten Generations as in (Deuteronomy 23: 2).

The curses are: Murderers (Cain's curse), children who strike their parents (Curse of Rebellion), kidnappers, those who curse their parents, abortion, witchcraft practitioners, those who sacrifice to fake gods. Also: Those who attempt to turn anyone away from the Lord, Those who follow horoscopes (astrology), Those who rebel against their pastors and leaders, False prophets, and women who do not remain virgins until they are married, Parents, who do not discipline their children, but honour them above God and Those who curse their rulers.

Teaching rebellion against God Refusing to warn sinners defiling the Sabbath Sacrificing human beings, participating in séances and fortune telling those involved in homosexual and lesbian relationships. Those who are Necromancers and fortune-tellers blaspheming the Lord's name. Those who are carnally minded those who practice sodomy and rebellious children. Those who are involved with occult e.g. fortune telling and palm reading. New Age e.g. yoga meditation only meditates on the word of God and not relies on hypnosis, and anything that blanks the mind. Board games e.g. ouiji boards, dungeons and dragons, snakes and ladders, and most of the computer games which people buy for their children. Martial arts as the culture are very saturated with demon worship.

In churches you could see a lot of fear, unbelief, rebellion, discord, strife, pride, spiritual death, witchcraft, the antichrist, infirmity, slumber death, splitting of churches, cancer, mind control, and lies. The spirit of lies usually comes after a traumatic incident takes place for example, physical accidents and Personal losses, Extreme embarrassment, fear, stress, or rejection.

One thing many people get trapped with is borrowing. The word of God says in (Proverbs 22:7),
*"The rich ruleth over the poor, and the borrower is servant to the lender."*

I am sure that as you read this book you can identify something that has affected you or someone you know who has fallen prey to borrowing. God has gotten rid of the curses on me and I know that he can do it for you too.

Over the centuries Satan has driven fear into hearts and the minds of Christians. Fear and superstitious ignorance keep us in bondage and these prevent us from acknowledging scriptural truths. This is because Satan jealously guards the secrets of his demonic kingdom. The ministry of deliverance is highly opposed and criticised. Rarely do people criticise the ministry of healing and or teaching the word of God on its own. We know that our Lord Jesus was often criticised much and was even accused of casting out devils by the power of Satan. Whatever the critics say or do to us we know that they did it to our Lord Jesus first.

## THE WASHING AND CLEANSING BY THE BLOOD OF JESUS

One night I was sleeping as usual and I was dreaming. In my dream two people came to get me and take me somewhere. As we were travelling I asked the people where they were taking me. One of them said to me that I was very filthy and my life needed cleansing with the blood of Jesus. They put me in what looked like a shower room and they showered my body with the blood of Jesus. I was jerking and shaking as if an electric current was being passed through my body. When I woke up the following morning I was still shaking vehemently. I did not take note of this incident until long after I was born again and delivered from the bondage of Satan.

In hindsight this incident reminded me of
(Zechariah 3:1-10):
*"Then he showed me Joshua the high priest standing before the Angel of the Lord and Satan standing at his right side to accuse him. The Lord said to Satan, "The Lord rebukes you Satan! The Lord who has chosen Jerusalem rebukes you! Is not this man a burning stick snatched from the fire?" Now Joshua was dressed in filthy clothes as he stood before the angel. The angel said to those who were standing before him, "Take off his filthy clothes." Then he said to Joshua, "See I have taken away your sin, and I will put rich garments on you." Then I said "put a clean turban on his head." So they put a clean turban on his head and clothed him, while the Angel of the*

*Lord stood by. The Angel of the Lord gave this charge to Joshua, "This is what the Almighty says", "If you walk in my ways and keep my requirements, then you will govern my house and have charge of my courts and I will give you a place among these standing here. Listen O High Priest Joshua and your associates seated before you, who are men of symbolic things to come. I am going to bring my servant the branch. See the stone I have set in front of Joshua! There are seven eyes on that one stone, and I will engrave an inscription on it, says the Lord God Almighty and I will remove the sin of this land in a single day. In that day each of you will invite his neighbour to sit under his vine or fig tree," declares the Lord Almighty."*

That was the beginning of my long road to deliverance.

I love the blood of Jesus and what the blood has done in my life. The blood of our Lord Jesus Christ is one of the most powerful tools at the disposal of the children of God. The blood of Jesus serves as atonement for our sins and it totally destroys demonic strong-holds. The blood of Jesus speaks better things than that of Abel's.

Abel's blood cried out for vengeance but the blood of Jesus pleads for forgiveness and restoration.

We who are in Christ Jesus have come to Jesus the mediator by way of a new and better covenant than the sprinkling of blood as in the days of Abel. In the Mosaic times God needed blood as atonement for sin. God ordered that and He needed it then. After He sent his only begotten son Jesus Christ to die for us on the cross there is no need for the blood of animal anymore. The blood of Jesus is the ultimate for achieving what God wants us to achieve. No animal sacrifice is needed anymore. The sacrifice with animals was temporal. The priests needed blood every time sin was committed. God now requires only the blood of Jesus.

There are still those who continue to sacrifice animals to appease evil spirits. You will see from what used to happen in my family why they used to kill animals and pour the blood of the animals over the entire yard. The elders needed to invoke the evil spirits so the spirits could do what they wanted to do. (Leviticus 17:11). Reads "For the life of the flesh is in the blood and I have given it for you for making atonement for you on the altar, for as for life it is the blood that makes atonement. (Hebrews 12:24) states that the blood of Jesus cleanses in the spirit and destroys the demons. No power of darkness can ever stand against the blood of Jesus Christ!

My very good friend and sister in Christ had a strange experience while I was in the middle of writing this book. She gave me permission to mention it in this book. She said to me that two policemen came to her door one night about eight thirty. She refused to open the door as it was late and she was alone in the house. The police persuaded her to open the door, which she finally did. They asked her if she was all right. She said that she was. They wanted to know who was with her in the house. She said that she was alone and that her son had gone to practise drumming. They indicated that they had received a phone call from her address saying that there was a pool of blood in her house. She replied that there was no blood in her house. The police insisted on checking her house to make sure that she was telling the truth. One of the policemen checked and saw that there was no blood in the house. They apologised and left.

When I went to her house she told me what had happened. As soon as she said that, I discerned that a witch had come to do some witchcraft in my friend's house but that the house was in fact covered with the blood of Jesus. The witch really did see the blood intact in the house, as most witches see things in the spirit realm. The blood caused the witch and she had to panic and this caused the witch to call the police emergency number.

My friend said to me that when she prays especially at night and she calls on the blood of Jesus and the fire of the Holy Spirit, something knocks at her window and begs her to stop putting fire on them. I told her to go to the police station and question them about that phone call because she was not at home at the time when all that happened. This she did. The police said to her that a phone call came at 14:30 hours to report that there was a pool of blood in her house. The police traced the phone call to her house. She said that she was not at work and her son was in school and she never made that phone call. They were puzzled.

We were aware of what happened in the Spirit realm and were rejoicing and praising God for the protection that He places on the believers and their property.

The blood of Jesus or the blood of the Lamb is the figurative expression for His atoning death. Blood represents life and life is so sacred before God. In the Mosaic Law the blood of the animals was used in all offerings for sin. Even the blood of wild beasts killed in the hunt or slaughtered for food was poured out and covered with earth. God did not want His people to drink blood. It was reserved for atonement purposes only. (Deuteronomy 12:15-16) says, "Never-the-less you may slaughter your animals in any of your towns and eat as much of the meat as you want, as if it were a gazelle or deer, according to the blessing the Lord your God gives eat it. But you must not eat the blood; pour it out on the ground like water." The blood of Jesus is sufficient to burn every devil in Satan's camp and to save every sinner on this earth. There is blood in heaven too. God sees only the blood of his son Jesus Christ. So we can go boldly to the throne of grace because of the blood of Jesus.

So the blood of Jesus started a big change in my life! Before I had no proper foundation in the Lord I did not even know who I was and I certainly had no understanding of what had happened in my dream except that I was in Christ. But the Lord God had other plans for my life, and they were good plans.

Even after I had that bizarre dream I did not know the ways of God or the significance of that dream. I used to keep many things to myself so I continued in my suffering. My ignorance was no defence as well. (Hosea 4:6) says,

**"My people are destroyed from lack of knowledge."**

The fact that I did not know that I had curses and evil influences in my life did not mean that the curses would not affect me. Satan and his demons were having a field day because they kept me in darkness. I did not realise that even the things that my forefathers had done would make me suffer like that. I did not believe that God would hold me responsible for things of which I was ignorant. I did not believe that I would be cursed if I did something wrong unknowingly. I did not know that God held me accountable for everything that is in his Word the Bible.

Read in your quiet time. (Leviticus 5:17), (Isaiah 27v11), (Jeremiah 6:19) and (Hosea 4: 6).

I did not know that to be born again is to wage war with Satan. I did not know that if you truly accept Jesus into your life Satan gets mad and will try to kill you. The battle is real and the casualties are real too. Have you ever noticed that when you live the ways of the world and come to Jesus, unexplained sickness, poverty, loss, shame and all sorts of inexplicable calamities happen to the Christians? Things go awry, awry. I used to wonder why? Now I know that before I was born again I belonged to Satan. As soon as I am born again I am of Jesus.

Satan fights to keep his people under His spell. He intimidates them like he used to do to me. He encumbered me with a lot of problems and I was so burned that I ended up backsliding. He also has an inherent right to persecute me. Man newly born again Christians lose their wealth etc., but God is a restorer. When God blesses you, you will be blessed and God will add no sorrow to your blessing.
THANK GOD FOR RADIO AND TV MINISTRIES

In England we have a Christian radio station called Premiere Radio. I started listening to the preaching on the Radio. It was like having church at home. One day I heard an African preacher. He did not have a good education and his grammar was poor. I was so caught up in criticising the grammar of that man that I man did no listen to most of the message. The bit I caught at the end seemed to be talking about me. I began to get angry with the man on the radio. How did he know what was happening in my life. I knew I did not tell anyone. Who was that man? In spite of this he seemed to be talking to me and about me. Little did I know that the man whose voice I hated so much would be my divine connection to my healing and deliverance. Now I have learnt not to look down on people because hey who knows who wil help you one day I began to wonder how that man knew the things that were happening to me in my life. I was unable to catch the phone number. That disturbed me very much.

The following Saturday my friend invited me to a prayer meeting. On reaching there we discovered that it was a leadership meeting so I decided to go back home, as I was not interested in being a leader. The people urged me to stay. I stayed and just listened but did not participate. At that meeting I met a nice man called Gunarm Singh He came up to me and said that he wanted to converse and pray with me. For some reason I assumed it was a prayer meeting. On the appointed day I went to the church to which he had invited me. When I reached there it was just he and a friend of his who were present. He has a powerful counselling ministry. He started by calling me a mighty woman of God. I was so amazed by that salutation because I certainly was not aware of it. He told me that I suffered domestic violence and how my husband was trying to kill me. He said how I could easily end up being a statistic. My ex husband had tried to kill me many times but God prevented him from doing so. I had a purpose in this life and I had to fulfil the purpose. He told me many confidential things. I was so broken hearted that I cried buckets of tears. The truth can be very painful but it needs to be told. In love. He prayed for me and encouraged me. I went for counselling with him for a few weeks. We dealt with different facets of my life every week and it was very hard to face myself. It was like opening a can of worms.

I was still in a pitiable state for a long time. He invited me to see his project for the homeless. I saw people who lived in the streets, and people who were worse off than me. I started helping him with his project. We would pray and I began to get stronger. At one point both Gurnam and I were listening to Premiere Radio at the same time

- 98 -

but we were at different places. When I went to see him I mentioned about the program I had heard on the radio and how the preacher seemed to be talking about me all the time. He said that when he was listening to that program the Lord told him to send me to that church for my deliverance. That was the place were I was going to get my deliverance.

As I write this book now Gurnam has gone to be with the Lord. He really had an impact in my walk with Jesus. The man had no children of his own. He adopted me and many other troubled people. I thank God for his life. This is an individual at whose death I felt at peace. Instead of mourning I kept thanking God for his life. So I got its phone number of the church and saved it in my mobile phone.

What used to happen to me is this, when I was among people I was fine and would think of nothing bad. When I was on my own I had suicidal thoughts. One day I felt particularly suicidal. I said to myself let me call the good Samaritans. I did. A man answered the phone. I said to him that I felt suicidal. He answered me in an angry voice and said why do I not do it quick and stop giving the world trouble. I was stunned into putting the phone down.

Another voice kept telling to call the church phone. I did. That was one of the best decisions I ever made in my life. Somebody on the other side of the phone asked me if I could drive and go there, I said yes. So at midnight on the 10th of February 2000, I drove myself to the Gilbert Deya Ministries in London. It was a long drive as I live in the opposite side of London. I want to thank God for Radio ministries, TV ministries and every other effective ministry. You make a big difference, and you are a lifeline when there is nowhere to turn to.

When I arrived at the ministry, Dee the receptionist gave me a very warm welcome. As I sat in the reception office the Man of God came to greet me but I did not recognize him. I did not realise that he was the one I had come to meet. He asked what I had come for; I said I had come to see Archbishop Gilbert Deya. He said to wait and we would soon see him. When my time to see him came I was so surprised to see the same man who had spoken to me at the reception was the one who was the archbishop. He was so happy to see me. I was so miserable and I could not understand why he was so happy. I did not understand why anybody could be that happy to see me. You know when you are miserable you do not understand why anyone should be happy. The happy people irritate you. He was talking to me as if he knew me very well. He was showing me some pictures of his family and telling me about his wife and children. He did all he could to make me feel comfortable. When I was more relaxed he listened to my problems. I explained everything that was bugging me. That day I left nothing out. He is a very good listener.

He took the phone and called a lady who was healed of polycystic liver and kidney problems. I was shocked to hear her testimony. As a nurse I knew that this disease is terminal and there is no way in which one can recover from it. I was so encouraged and amazed.

After the talk I was expecting the Archbishop to pray a long prayer and do something extraordinary. He did not pray at all. He just looked me straight in my eyes and said to me "Woman you have a lot of demons in you. You are also carrying the burdens people have long since been dead that is why you have all those problems." I did not know what demons were. I also did not understand how I could carry the burdens of the dead people in my family, but I believed him. I am a very curious person. I really wanted to know how anybody could carry the burdens of those who had passed away. In listening to the teachings of the archbishop I learnt about generational curses. As I explained before, my family were warriors.

I originate from the tribe of Chaka Zulu. So you see my great grandparents were not God-fearing people. They were in to killing, witchcraft, and all sorts of ancestral and demonic cults. This was why I was so burned. The spirit that ruled in the family was the same that affected every generation. I now know that these spirits had no more effect on me. I have repented as you will see in one of the later chapters. I now make it my duty to teach others about what ignorance can do to you. I am the fourth generation who was carrying the burdens of my dead relatives. Now there is no more pleasing the dead. It is finished! Jesus became a curse for me to be set free from generational curses. I also became aware of doorways that can open you to demonic influences.

What he said to me witnessed in my spirit when he said it. Initially I knew that my life was not right with God but I did not know what it was amiss. I was happy in my heart with what the man of God said. I knew I had problems but I did not know the source of these problems.

I believe that when you have a problem and you know that you have that problem, fifty percent of that problem is solved. When you get the right help then it is seventy-five per cent solved when you follow the right advice or the prescription then one hundred per cent of the problem will be solved. It is very hard to fight an enemy you do not know exists. Now I knew my enemy was demons and generational curses. ALL THESE YEARS I HAD LIVED WITH THEM AND DID NOT KNOW THAT I WAS POSSESED BY THE DEVIL AND THAT I WAS CURSED.

He advised me to go to deliverance sessions. Please note that a curse is broken in the name of Jesus. Demons are cast out in the name of Jesus!

ARE YOU IN THE CHURCH YET YOU ARE DEMON-POSSESSED?

My circumstances remind me of the man in (Mark 1:21-26). They went to Capernaum and when the Sabbath came, Jesus went into the synagogue and began to teach. The people were amazed at His teaching, because he taught as one who had authority not as the teachers of the law. Just then a man in their synagogue who was possessed by an evil spirit cried out "What do you want with us Jesus of Nazareth? Have you come to destroy us? I know who you are the Holy one of God!" "Be quiet!" said Jesus sternly "come out of him" the evil spirit shook the man violently and came out of him with a shriek. The people were so amazed that they asked each other.

What is this? A new teaching with authority He even gives orders to evil spirits and they obey him. Can this be you sitting in church, but some problems are overwhelming you? Could you be demonised and you are not aware of it? Could a curse be operative in your life and your family's life, and you do not know of it? What is a curse? What is a demon? How do I know that I have a demon within my body? How do I know that I have a curse in my life? Let me try to explain.

WHAT IS A CURSE?

TO CURSE IS TO USE PROFANELY INSOLENT LANGUAGE AGAINST, TO CALL UPON DIVINE OR SUPERNATURAL POWER TO SEND INJURY UPON, TO EXECRATE IN FERVENT OFTEN PROFANE TERMS, TO BRING GREAT EVIL UPON, TO AFFLICT.
A CURSE IS A BAD PRAYER OR INVOCATION FOR HARM OR INJURY TO COME UPON SOMEONE. IT IS AN EVIL OR MISFORTUNE THAT COMES AS A RESULT OF AN N IMPRECATION OR AS RETRIBUTION. IT CAUSES GREAT HARM AND MISFORTUNE IN THE RECIEPIENT'S LIFE. THE REASON TO PLACE A CURSE N SOMEONE IS TO CAUSE HARM AND DESTRUCTION.

MANY PEOPLE HAVE ACTUALLY LOST THEIR LIVES AS A RESULT OF CURSES. WHOLE FAMILY LINES CAN BE CLOSED BECAUSE OF A CURSE. COUNTRIES, CONTINENTS, LEADERS, CHURCHES CAN BE CURSED TOO.
WHAT IS A DEMON?

A DEMON IS AN UNCLEAN SPIRIT AND ALSO AN EVIL SPIRIT IT CAN BE KNOWN AS A DEVIL. DIFFERENT VERSIONS CALL THEM DIFFERENT NAMES. THEY ARE ALSO KNOWN AS THE GODS OF THE HEATHEN; THEY

ARE THE SPIRITS BEHIND THE IDOLS THEY ARE SPIRITUAL BEINGS, IN REBELLION AGANST GOD, HAVING THE POWER TO LEAD MEN INTO SIN AND AFFLICT THEM WITH DISEASE. APPARENTLY THOSE POSSESED  HAD NEARLY LOST ALL POWER OF WILL. POSSESSION BY DEMONS FREQUENTLY LEADS TO BODILY DISEASE OR INSANITY.

WHO CAN CURSE YOU AND WHY?

A CURSE CAN COME FROM SATAN  LEGALLY OR ILLEGALLY THE PURPOSE OF THIS IS TO INJURE, TO CAUSE LOSS OR TO DESTROY OR KILL.

THE CURSE THAT COMES FROM GOD IS TO GAIN THE PERSON' S ATTENTION .HE NEEDS TO TURN FROM HIS EVIL WAYS TO GOD AND WALK IN THE RIGHT WAYS OF GOD. IF THE PERSON IS HARD HEARTED GOD CAN KILL THE PERSON OR ALLOW SATAN TO DESTROY THAT PERSON.

As an example, after King Solomon had finished dedicating the temple that he had built for the Lord in (2 Chronicles 7:12-22). God is warning Solomon that God would send a curse to His people if they do not walk according to his prescribed ways. God himself was going to do it. The Lord appeared to him to him at night and said; "I have heard your prayer and I have chosen this place for myself as a temple for sacrifices. When I shut the heavens so that there is no rain, or command the locusts to devour the land or send a plague among my people. If my people, who are called by my name, will humble themselves and pray and seek my face and turn from their wicked ways then I will hear from heaven and will forgive their sin and will heal their land. Now my eyes will be open and my ears attentive to the prayers offered in this place. I have chosen and consecrated this temple so that my name will be there forever. My eyes and my heart will always be there. As for you if you walk before me as David your father did, and do all I command, and observe my laws and decrees. I will establish your royal throne, as I have covenanted with David your father when I said you shall never fail to have a man rule over Israel. But if you turn away and forsake the decrees and commands I have given you and go off to serve other gods and worship them, then I will uproot Israel from my land, which I have given them, and will reject this temple, which I have consecrated for my Name. I will make it a byword and an object of ridicule among all peoples. And though this temple is so imposing all who pass by will be appalled and say, 'Why has the Lord done such a thing to this land and to this temple?' People will answer, 'They have forsaken the Lord the God of their fathers, who brought them out of Egypt, and have embraced other gods, worshipping and serving them-that is why he brought all this disaster upon them."

## A CURSE THAT CAME FROM SATAN WITH LEGAL GROUNDS

(Joshua 7) talks about Achan's sin and how thirty-six innocent men died. The culprit Achan was responsible for the death of his family because of his greed. When Achan was stealing, God and Satan saw him. We can learn from this to refrain, bringing items that are devoted to the idol worship as that will give them the legal right to attack the household of the person who does it. I will quote from (Joshua 7:3-24). When they returned to Joshua, they said,

> *"Not all the people will have to go up against Ai. Send two to three thousand men to take it and do not weary all the people, for only a few men are there. So about three thousand men went up, but the men of Ai routed them. Who killed about thirty-six of them? They chased the Israelites from the city gates as far to the stone quarries and struck them down on the slopes. At this the hearts of the people melted and became like water. Then Joshua tore his clothes and fell face down to the Lord before the ark of the Lord, remaining there until evening.*
>
> *The elders of Israel did the same and sprinkled dust on their heads. And Joshua said "Oh sovereign Lord God, why did you ever bring*

*this people across the Jordan to deliver us into the hands of the Amorites to destroy us? If only we had been content to stay on the other side of the Jordan!*

*O Lord what can I say now that Israel has been routed by its enemies? The Canaanites and the other people of the country will hear about this and they will surround us and wipe out our name from the earth. What then will you do for your own great name?"*

*The Lord said to Joshua, "Stand up! What are you doing on your face? Israel has sinned; they have violated my covenant, which I commanded them to keep. They have taken some of the devoted, they have stolen, they have lied, and they have put them in their own possessions. That is why the Israelites cannot stand against their enemies; they turn their backs and run because they have been made liable to destruction. For this is what the Lord, the God of Israel, says that which is devoted among you is devoted to destruction. I will not be with you anymore unless you destroy whatever among you is devoted to destruction. Go consecrate the people.*

*Tell them; consecrate yourselves in preparation for tomorrow, for this is what the lord God the God of Israel says. That which is devoted is among you, o Israel. You cannot stand against your enemies unless you remove it.*

*"In the morning present yourself tribe by tribe. The tribe that the lord shall take shall come forward clan by clan. The clan that the lord takes shall come forward family by family, and the family that the Lord takes shall come forward man by man. He who is caught wit the devoted things shall be destroyed by fire along with all that belongs to him. He has violated the covenant of the lord and has done a disgraceful thing in Israel. Early the next morning Joshua had Israel come forward by tribes, and Judah came forward, and he took the Zerahites. He had the clan of the Zerahites come forward by families, and Zimri was taken. Joshua had his family come forward man by man, and Achan son of Carmi the son of Zimri, the son of Zerah, of the tribe of Judah, was taken. Then Joshua said to Achan, My son give glory to the Lord the God of Israel, and gives him the praise. Tell me what you have done do not hide it from me. Achan replied, It is true I have sinned against the Lord the God of*

*Israel. This is what I have done. When I saw in the plunder a beautiful robe from Babylonia, two hundred shekels of silver, and a wedge of gold weighing fifty shekels, I coveted them and took them. They are hidden in the ground inside my tent, with the silver underneath. So Joshua sent messengers and they ran to the tent and there it was, hidden in his tent and the silver underneath. They took the things from the tent brought them to Joshua and all the Israelites and spread them out before the Lord. Then Joshua together with all Israel took Achan son of Zerah, the silver, the robe, the gold wedge, his sons and daughters, his cattle donkey's sheep, his tent and all that he had, to the valley of Achor. Joshua said why have you brought this trouble on us? The Lord will bring trouble on you today. Then all Israel stoned him, and after they had stoned the rest, they burned them. Over Achan they heaped a large pile of rocks, which remains to this day. Then the Lord turned from his fierce anger. Therefore that place has been called the valley of Achor ever since."*

You see, what really annoys and upsets me is that Achan was doing all this without the knowledge or permission of his family. Innocent wives, children and livestock were killed for something of which they were not aware. What can we say? God is just! Who can ask him what He is doing? He is God! Look at what happened when God punished Achan. He and his entire family were put to death. That rule of God is still effective today. Some of you are so good and true to God and yet you suffer so much. Usually it is the good people who suffer so much why? It could be that your father could be an Achan. Fathers, what secret sins have you done to get your children in these terrible circumstances? Mothers, some things you have done in your youth will still affect your children unto the third and fourth generation unless you repent and break those curses that came with them. The stone is no longer physically thrown, but what about the spiritual stones that are being thrown to you and your children Drug addiction, premature deaths, mental sicknesses, incurable diseases Divorce, strife, poverty, lack, bad luck, lack of fulfilment in life and other bad things that can happen in life.

In the Old Testament they had a test for an unfaithful wife. In (Numbers 5:11-29) the Lord said to Moses.

*"Speak to the Israelites and say to them. If a man's wife goes astray and is unfaithful to him by sleeping with another man, and this is hidden from her husband and her impurity is undetected (since there is no witness against her and she has not been caught in the act) and if the feelings of jealousy came over her husband and he suspects that his wife is impure or if he is jealous and suspects her even if she is not impure, then he is to take his wife to the priest. He must take an offering of a tenth of an ephah of barley flour on her behalf. He must also take an offering of a tenth of an ephah of barley on her behalf. He must not pour oil on it or put incense in it, because it is a grain offering of jealousy - a reminder offering to draw attention to guilt. The priest shall bring her and have her stand before the Lord. Then he shall take some holy water in a clay jar and put some dust from the tabernacle floor into the water. After the priest has had the woman stand before the Lord, he shall loosen her hair and place in her hands the reminder offering for jealousy, while he himself holds the bitter water that brings a curse. Then the priest shall put the woman under oath and say to her, if no other man has slept with you and you have not gone astray, and become impure while married to your husband, may this water that brings a curse, not harm you. But if you have gone astray while married to your husband, you have defiled yourself by sleeping with a man other than your husband, here the priest is to put the woman under this curse of the oath, may the Lord cause your people to curse and denounce you, when he causes your thigh to waste away and your abdomen to swell. May this water that brings a curse enter your body so that your abdomen swells and your thigh wastes away? The woman is to say Amen, so be it.*

*The priest is then to write these curses on a scroll and then wash them off into the bitter water. He shall have the woman drink the bitter water. He shall have the woman drink the bitter water that brings a curse, and this water will enter into her and cause bitter suffering. The priest is then to take a handful of the grain offering for jealousy, wave it before the Lord, and bring it to the altar. The priest is then to take a handful of the grain offering as a memorial offering and burn it on the altar. After that he is to have the woman drink the water.  If she has defiled herself and has been unfaithful to her husband, then when she is made to drink the water that brings a curse, it will go into her and cause her bitter suffering, her abdomen will swell and her thigh will waste away, and she will become accursed among her people.  If however, the woman has not defiled herself and is free from impurity, she will be cleared of guilt and will be able to have children."*

## DO THESE THINGS HAPPEN TODAY? WE ARE NO LONGER IN THOSE OLD DAYS!

These laws are still applicable today.  We are no longer under the old Mosaic Law.  Jesus fulfilled the law and set us free under the New Covenant by His blood.  However, the spiritual principles laid down for the children of Israel in the Old Testament still hold true in our lives today.

Mum what did you do?  What is causing your bitter suffering today?  Sister what is it that is bringing a curse in your life?  Have you had an extramarital affair?

Your husband might never know but God saw you.  Satan and his demons saw it too.  That is why things are going wrong in your life.  Your death might not be physical, but it is spiritual swelling the thigh swelling of the abdomen?  The doctors might not be able to see the problem, this is not witchcraft.  This is the swelling of the abdomen as it is in the scripture in the part dealing with spiritual wasting of the thigh Bitter suffering shame of being accursed among your own people eating and never being satisfied. Bitterness, disappointments and a lot of other negative stuff.

Do people look down on you and laugh at you and hate you for no reason whatever?  Why, you? Why?

If you are impure that means that you are dirty inside. No amount of soap and water can cleanse you. Only the blood of Jesus and the repenting and confession of your sins can help!

I now address men: What you did can also affect your children unto the third and fourth generation. Also unnecessary jealousy is bad. You could drive your wives to do things that are inimical to a healthy marriage. Men should trust and love their wives God is able to keep your partner and make them faithful to you. A marriage that has no trust in it is doomed to failure. If you have jealous thoughts, take it to the Lord Jesus and He will cure you of it. Extreme jealousy is a curse. It just drives your partner crazy. It is self-destructive. It can kill.
See (Songs of Solomon 8:6). It reads,
> *"Place me like a seal over your heart, like a seal on your arm, for love is strong as death, its jealousy unyielding as the grave. It burns like a blazing fire, like a mighty flame."*

Extreme anger is very bad. It is acceptable to have righteous anger, as Jesus Himself became angry on certain occasions. You could be the descended of a family that has done terrible things. The sad thing is that no one may have told you what evil curses had been laid on you. You only find out when things have gone so bad that the problems are so tremendous that they lead you to God whether you like it or not. Some mothers have been having an affair with more than one man and then when they get pregnant, they do not know whom their father is. These children go through the mill.

I was in the hairdressers once and a woman was complaining. She said she had so many problems with her son; the son was beating her up and verbally abusing her. She said that she had not told the father that he had a son with her and another man was raising the son as his own. Her friend was advising her to take the boy to his real father so that her problems would cease. I have a cousin who had a child with another man while she was married to her husband. The daughter had lots of problems as she grew up. She became suicidal. Many times she took tablets to kill herself. The mother then decided to come clean and revealed who the real father was. She took the girl to her real father and she is now mentally stable.

As for some of you, your forefathers did abominable things to God that has not been sincerely repented for. As long as you do not repent the problems will continue to cause havoc in your life. The question that some of you are asking is
"WHY ME?"  I used to ask myself that all the time, Why me?  Why is it that if any bad thing happened, it always happened to me?

THE CURSE THAT COMES FROM SATAN USES THE DEMONS TO BRING ABOUT THE FULFILMENT OF THAT CURSE. EACH TIME IN THE BIBLE IF THE NATION OF ISRAEL SINNED AND DID NOT REPENT, GOD SENT INVADING ARMIES OF FOREIGN NATIONS TO DESTROY THEM.
(Proverbs 26:2) says,
*"Like a fluttering sparrow or a darting swallow, an undeserved curse does not come to rest."*

Note in this reading that the children of Israel and Balaam were worshipping their God and going about their business.  As long as they were going according to the will of God nothing bad happened to them.  Their enemies were terrified of them. When you walk right with God your enemies are afraid of you.  Nothing will happen to you unless God himself allows it to happen.  Please note what these three chapters say.

(Numbers 22 – 24) says,
*"Then the Israelites travelled to the Plains of Moab and camped along the Jordan across from Jericho. Now Balak son of Zippor saw all that the Israel done to the Amorites, and Moab was terrified because they were so many people.  Indeed Moab was filled with dread because of the Israelites.  The Moabites said to the elders of Midian, 'this horde is going to lick up everything around us, as an ox licks up the grass of the fields', so Balak son of Zippor who was*

king of Moab at that time, sent messengers to summon Balaam son of Beor who was at Pethor, near the river, in his native land.

Balak said 'a people has come out of Egypt, they cover the face of the land and have settled next to me. Now come and put a curse on these people, because they are too powerful for me. Perhaps than ill be able to defeat them and drive them out of the country. For I know that those who you bless are blessed and those who you curse are cursed.'

The elders of Moab and Midian left, taking with them the fee for divination. When they came to Balaam, they told him what Balak had said. 'Spend the night here' Balaam said to them, and I will bring you back the answer the Lord gives me. So the Moabite princes stayed with him.
God came to Balaam, and asked, 'who are these men with you?' Balaam said to God 'Balak son of Zippor, king of Moab, send me this message. A people who have came out of Egypt covers the face of the land: Now come and put a curse on them. Perhaps then ill be to fight them and drive then away'. But God said to Balaam, 'do not go with them. You must not put a curse on those people because they are blessed'. The next morning Balaam got up and said to Balak's princes, 'go back to your own country for the Lord has refused to let me go with you'.

So the Moabite princes returned to Balak and said 'Balaam refused to come with us'. Then Balak sent other princes more numerous and more distinguished than the first. They came to Balaam and said 'this is what Balak son of Zippor says do not let anything keep you from coming to me, because I will reward you handsomely and do whatever you say. Come and put a curse on these people'.

But Balaam answered then 'even if Balak gave me his palace filled silver and gold, I could not do anything great or small to go beyond the command of the Lord my God. Now stay here tonight as the others did, and I will find out what else the Lord will tell me'. That *night the Lord came to Balaam 'since these men have come to summon you, go with them but do only what I tell you'.*

*Balaam got up in the morning saddled his donkey and went with the princes of Moab. But God was very angry when he went and the Angel of the Lord stood in the road to oppose him. Balaam was riding on his donkey and his two servants were with him. When the donkey saw the Angel of the Lord standing in the road with a drawn sword in his hand, she turned of the road into a field. Balaam beat her to get her onto the road. Then the Angel of the Lord stood in a narrow path between the two vineyards, with walls on both sides.*

*When the donkey saw the Angel of the Lord she pressed close to the walls, crushing Balaam's foot against it. So he beat her again. Then the Angel of the Lord moved on ahead and stood in a narrow place where there was no room to turn, either to the right or the left. When the donkey saw the Angel of the Lord she lay down under Balaam, and he was angry and beat her with his staff. Then the Lord opened the donkey's mouth and she said to Balaam 'what have I done to you to make you beat me these three times?'*

*Balaam answered the donkey, 'you have made a fool of me! If I had a sword in my hand I would kill you right now'. The donkey said to Balaam 'am I not your own donkey which you have always ridden till this day? Have I been in the habit of doing this to you?' 'No' he said. Then the Lord opened Balaam's eyes and he saw the Angel of the Lord standing in the road with his sword drawn. So he bowed low and fell face down. The Angel of the Lord asked him, 'why have you beaten your donkey three times? I have come here to oppose you because your path is reckless before me. The donkey saw me and turned away from me these three times. If she had not turned away I would certainly have killed you by now, but I would have spared her'. Balaam said to the Angel of the Lord, 'I have sinned'. I did not realise you were standing in the road to oppose me. Now if you are displeased, I will go back'. The Angel of the Lord said to Balaam 'go with the men, but speak only what I tell you'. So Balaam went with the princes of Balak.*

When Balak heard that Balaam was coming, he went out to meet him at the Moabite town on the Arnon boarder, at the edge of his territory. Balak said to Balaam 'Did I not send you an agent summons, why didn't you come to me? Am I really not able to reward you'?

'Well I have come to you now' Balaam replied. But can I just say anything I must speak only what God puts in my mouth. Then Balaam went with Balak Kiriath Huzoth. Balak sacrificed Cattle and sheep, and gave some to Balaam and the princes who were with him. The next morning Balak took Balaam to Bamoth Baal, and from there he saw part of the people."

Balaam said build me seven altars here, and prepare seven altars here, and prepare seven bulls and seven rams for me. Balak did as Balaam said and the two of them offered a bull and a ram on each altar.

Then Balaam said to Balak 'stay here beside you offering while I go aside. Perhaps the Lord will come to meet with me. Whatever he reveals to me I will tell you'. Then he went of to a barren height. God met with him, and Balaam said 'I have prepared seven altars and on each altar I have offered a bull and a ram'.

The Lord put a message in Balaam's mouth and said, 'go back to Balak and give him this message'. So he went back to him and found him standing besides his offering, with all the princes of Moab. Then Balaam uttered his oracle 'Balak brought me from Aram, the king of Moab from the eastern mountains. Come he said curse Jacob for me, come, denounce Israel. How can I curse whom God has not cursed? How can denounce those whom the Lord has not denounced? From the rock peaks I see them. Form the heights I view them. I see a people who live apart and do not consider themselves one of the nations who can count the dust of Jacob or number the forth part of Israel? Let me die the death of the righteous and may my end be like theirs!'

*Balak said to Balaam 'what have you done to me? I brought you to curse my enemies, but you have done nothing but bless them!' He answered must I not speak what the Lord puts in my mouth*

*Then Balak said come with me to anther place where you can see them. And from there curse them for me. So he took him to the field of Zophim on the top of Pisgah, and there he built seven altars and offered a bull and a ram on each altar. Balaam said to Balak 'stay here beside you offering while I meet with him over there' the Lord met with Balaam and put a message in Balaam's mouth and said 'go back to Balak and give him this message'. So he went to him and found him standing besides his offering with the princes of Moab. Balak asked him 'what did the Lord say?'*

*Then he uttered this oracle 'arise Balak and listen, hear me, son of Zippor God is not man that he should lie or a son of man that he should change his mind. Does He speak and then not act? Does He promise and not fulfil? I have received a command to bless, He has blessed and I cannot change it. No misfortune is seen in Jacob, no misery observed in Israel. The Lord their God is with them, the shout of the king is among them, God brought them out of Egypt they have the strength of a wild ox. There is no sorcery against Jacob, no divination against Israel. It will now be said of Jacob and of Israel, see what God has done! The people rise like a lioness they rouse themselves like a lion that does not rest till he devours his prey and drinks the blood of his victims of his victims'. Then Balak said to Balaam 'either curse them or bless them at all' Balaam answered, 'did I not tell you I must do whatever the Lord says'.*
*Then Balak said to Balaam 'come let me take you to another place'. Perhaps it will please God to let you curse them for me there. And Balak took Balaam to the top of Peor, overlooking the wasteland. Balaam said build me seven alters here, and prepare seven bulls and seven rams for me. Balak did as Balaam said, and offered a bull and a ram on each alter.*

*Now when Balaam saw that it pleased the Lord to bless Israel he did not resort to sorcery as at other times, but turned his face towards* the desert. When Balaam looked out and saw Israel en camped tribe by tribe, the spirit of God came upon him and he uttered his oracle.

The oracle of Balaam son Beor, the oracle of one whose eye sees clearly, the oracle of one who hears the words of God, who sees, a vision from the all mighty who falls prostrate, and whose eyes are opened. How beautiful are your tents, O, Jacob, your dwelling places, O Israel! Like valleys the spread out, like gardens beside a river, like aloes planted by the Lord, like cedars besides the waters. Water will flow form their buckets; there seeds will have abundant water. Their king will be greater than Agag; their kingdom will be exalted. God bought them out of Egypt; they have strength of a wild ox. They devour hostile nations and break their bones in pieces; with their arrows they pierce them. Like a lion the crouch and lie down like a lioness who dares to rouse them? May those who bless you be blessed and those who curse you be cursed.

Then Balak's anger burned against Balaam's. He struck his hands together and said to him, 'I summoned you to curse my enemies but you have blessed them theses three times. Now leave at once and go home! I said I would reward you handsomely, but the Lord has kept you from being rewarded'. Balaam answered Balak 'Did I not tell the messengers you sent me, even if Balak gave me his palace filled with silver and gold, I could not do anything of my own accord, good or bad, to go beyond the command of the Lord – and I must say only what the Lord says? Now I am going back to my people, but come, let me warn you of what these people will do to your people in days to come'.
Then he made this pronouncement, 'The oracle of Balaam son of Beor, the oracle of one you eye sees clearly, the oracle of one who hears the word of God, who has knowledge of the most high who sees a vision from the almighty, who falls prostrate', and who's eyes are opened. I see him, but not now, I behold him, but not near.

A star will come out of a Jacob; a sceptre will rise out of Israel. He will crush the foreheads of Moab, the skulls of all the sons of Sheath. Edom will be conquered, Seir, his enemy will be conquered, *but Israel will grow strong. A ruler will come out of Jacob and destroy the survivors of the city'.*

*Then Balaam saw Amalek and uttered his oracle. Amalek was first among the nations, but he will come to ruin at last. Then he saw the Kenites and uttered his oracle your dwelling place is secured, your nest is set in a rock, yet you Kenites will be destroyed when Asshur takes you captive. Then he uttered his oracle. Ah, who can live when God does this? Ships will come from the shores of Kittim, they will subdue Asshur and Eber, but they too will come to ruin. Then Balaam got up and returned home, and Balak went on his own way.*

## HOW DO I KNOW THAT I HAVE DEMONS? HOW CAN I TELL THAT I HAVE A CURSE OVER MY LIFE?

First of all I did not know that those things existed until a Man of God who has a discerning spirit made me aware of them. I could have said, "No thank you very much I do not have them." I did not see them but my life was going wrong. I had no control of what was happening in my life. I decided to humble myself and find out as much as I could about them. I have the best manuscript - the Bible.

Here is what the Word of God says in
(Deuteronomy 28:15- 48),
" *However if you do not obey the Lord your God and do not carefully follow all his commands and decrees I am giving you today, all these curses will come upon you. You will be cursed in the city and in the country.*
*Your basket and your kneading trough will be cursed. The fruit of your womb will be cursed, the crops of your land, and the calves of your herds and the lambs of your flocks. You will be cursed when you come in and you will be cursed when you go out. The Lord will send curses on you, and cause confusion and rebuke in everything you put your hand to, until you are destroyed and come to a sudden ruin because of the evil you have done in forsaking Him.*"
*The Lord will plague you with diseases until he has destroyed you from the land you are entering to possess. The Lord will strike you with wasting disease, with fever and inflammation, with scorching heat and drought, with blight and mildew, which will plague you until you perish. The sky over your head will be bronze, the ground beneath you iron.*

*The Lord will turn the rain of your country into dust and powder; it will come down from the skies until you are destroyed. The Lord will cause you to be defeated before your enemies. You will come at them from one direction but flee from them in seven, and you will become a thing of horror to all the kingdoms of the earth. Your carcases will be food to the all the birds of the air and the beasts of the earth, and there will be no one to frighten them away.*

*The Lord will afflict you with boils of Egypt and with tumours, festering sores and the itch, from which you cannot be cured. The Lord will afflict you with madness, blindness and confusion of mind. At midday you will grope about like a blind man in the dark. You will be unsuccessful in everything you do; day after day you will be oppressed and robbed, with no one to rescue you.*

*You will be pledged to be married to a woman, but another man will take her and ravish her. You will build a house but you will not live in it. You will plant a vineyard but will not even begin to enjoy its fruit. Your ox will be slaughtered before you own eyes, but you will eat none of it. Your donkey will be forcibly taken from you and will not be returned. Your sheep will be giving to your enemies, and no one will rescue them.*

*Your sons and daughters will be given to another nation; and you will wear your eyes watching for them day after day, powerless to lift a hand. A people that you do not know will eat what your land and labour produce, and you will have nothing but cruel oppression all your days. The sight you see will drive you mad. The Lord will afflict your knees and legs with painful boils that cannot be cured, spreading from the soles of your feet to the top of your head.*

*The Lord will drive you and the king you set over you to a nation unknown to you or your fathers. There you will worship other gods, gods of wood and stone. You will become a thing of horror an object of scorn and ridicule to all the nations where the Lord will drive you.*

*You will sow much seed in the field but you will harvest a little, because the locusts will devour it. You will plant vineyards and cultivate them, but you will not drink the wine or gather the grapes, because worms will them. You will have olive trees throughout your country but you will not use the oil, because the olives will drop off. You will have sons and daughters but you will not keep them, because they will go into captivity. Swarms of locusts will take over all your trees and the crops of your land.*

*The alien who lives among you will rise above you higher and higher, but you will sink lower and lower. He will lend to you, but you will not lend to him. He will be the head and you will be the tail.*

*All these curses will come upon you. They will pursue you and overtake you until you are destroyed, because you did not obey the lord your god and observe the commandments and decrees he gave you. They will be a wonder to you and your descendants forever. Because you did not serve the Lord your God joyfully and gladly in the time of prosperity, therefore in hunger in thirst, in nakedness and dire poverty, you will serve the enemies the Lord sends against you. He will put an iron yoke on your neck until he has destroyed you.*

You see all these are curses and they happen to believers, who are not walking right with God.
Is your life or the life of your family plagued with premature deaths?
Strife Tragedies Divorce
Perversion  Incest Incurable disease
Funny illnesses Poverty Lack Suicide
Alcoholism Prostitution Destruction
Mental illness is your country going through a famine Recession War Atrocities? Violence
Poverty Spiritual dryness Unrest and oppression
 Is your church going through splitting?
Not prospering?  Not growing spiritually?
Lots of sicknesses and deaths of the members
Unbelief Rebellion Often changing pastors going round in circles?
Spiritual death
Mind control? Teaching the wrong doctrine?

If these things are happening then there could be a possibility that a curse has been placed. The good news is Jesus can break any curse. He became the curse so that we might be blessed. Earlier on in the Chapter, the Lord talks about blessings. In order to be blessed you have to live in the ways prescribed by God. There are consequences for obedience and by the same token there are consequences for disobedience.

- 119 -

# CHAPTER 10

## MY DELIVERANCE IN INDIA

### THE BEGINNING OF MY DELIVERANCE

From what I have shared with you, you can tell that my life was plagued with curses and that I was demonised. After the counselling with the Archbishop I decided to go for deliverance sessions.

I starting going for the deliverance. I did not know what to expect or what to do. As I walked in the deliverance room, I started to vomit violently. I just ran to the nearest bin to let up there. I was so amazed as I was feeling no nausea or sickness.

I was coughing, choking and splattering for a very long time. I spent at least two hours with my head in the bin. I have never vomited and coughed like that in all my life. I had no control over myself. I felt so ashamed because I had just walked into that place and was behaving like that. It was not very nice.

I thought that some thing like this had never happened to me before. I became convinced that this was because I was emotionally wound up and that I had drunk lots of tea that morning. I told myself that I would not eat nor drink anything the following morning. I was so tired from the retching and all that coughing and splattering. Afterwards I was unable to drive home so I slept in my car for about two hours.

The following day I was determined not to behave in such a manner so I went to the session on an empty stomach. I managed to walk to the front of the room. I wanted to see everything that was happening and not miss a thing.

When the prayers started, a clear voice was telling me to look at a certain lady. I looked at the lady in question. The voice said to me I should not go anywhere near her as she would torture me. I complied with what the voice had told me. Later on I discovered that the lady in question was a spirit-filled deliverance minister. That made me realise that demons can speak to you. They are also aware of the anointed servants of God. They have intellect. They get tired. They have memories, they investigate they walk they panick and they fear Jesus. They knew Paul. They knew Jesus. They know the anointed men and women of God.

I kept well way from the minister as much as I could. The Spirit of God for deliverance made its presence felt very strong in the room. As the minister was commanding the devils to come out I heard myself screaming and frightened, my body was shaking and I was vomiting and choking violently. I was swearing and kicking. It took about five people to pin me down.

Now I am a very small woman and in the natural there is no way I could fight big people like that. It could only happen by demonic influence.

I was so confused and ashamed, as I did not understand how I became so violent. I quickly left the room soon after the session. I did not wait for an explanation I just wanted to go home. I was so embarrassed and confused. I had no strength left in me I had to sleep in my car for at least two hours.

On my way home I vowed never to go back there again. Two voices were speaking to me. One was saying, "You really made a fool of yourself today. We told you not to go to that church but you did not listen now look at the shame you brought to yourself." The other voice was saying to me, "you need to go back. This is how you will get your deliverance." I have never been so confused!

After a good night's sleep, I woke up refreshed. The voice that was telling me not to go had been silent. The voice that said to me to go was speaking. I decided to go back to the deliverance room. There is power of deliverance in this room.

This time I was manifesting as a snake. They were casting out the serpentine spirit out of me. I was lying flat on my belly and hissing like a snake. I manifested in different animal forms - for example a dog, a bird, a leopard, a lion and other different animals.

At one point I was manifesting as a mermaid. I was so confused when I woke up. I could hear the deliverance minister casting out the mermaid spirit out of my life. I wondered how I got that spirit. I remember my mum telling me that when she was a little girl she went to the river in her village to fish. She was alone. When she was fishing she looked up and saw a white woman with a fish tail come towards her. My mum started to move backwards and the thing was coming towards her. She screamed and kept going but backwards so she could see the thing that was coming towards her. Then as suddenly as it appeared, it disappeared and went back in the water. I am convinced something happened between my mum and that spirit. I happened to inherit it. I phoned my mum in Zimbabwe and asked her about the incident and she confirmed it.

Sometimes I would blackout and not know what had happened to me. Some people used to tell me that when I was out like that, a male guttural voice would be speaking through me and I would be fighting with the deliverance ministers. The more I went for the deliverance sessions, the more I started to feel better in my body.

Fear was one of the first spirits to go. Confusion left I started to get stronger and stronger. Sorrow went. Pity partying stopped. I started to smile again. My countenance changed, I looked better, many people were remarking on how well I looked. My friends told me that my face had aged and that the colour of my visage also changed. I had gone into premature menopause at the age of twenty-four but after the deliverance sessions my period returned. But the Good Lord restored me back to normalcy again. All the Glory belongs unto Him!

The ministers told me that I needed to keep coming for more deliverance sessions. They did not tell me how many more sessions I had to attend.

I was going through deliverance sessions for a long time. Many individuals who came after me were being pronounced delivered, but in my case I was not. I was getting tired of attending those sessions and sometimes jealous of those who came after me, and were being delivered before I was. Even though in some ways things were getting better in my body, in other way things were worsening.

One day I was going to work, I felt a sharp slap across my face. A human hand had slapped me across the face. I felt it but I did not see it. When I arrived at my place of work my left eye was swollen. My colleagues told me to go home. As soon as I reached home I called the ministry. The Archbishop happened to answer my call. He told me to go to the ministry immediately. He said he had seen some spirits that been sent to kill me. He advised me to get a mini cab. I rushed down to the ministry. As soon as I arrived there two eminent pastors started to cast those spirits out of me. Pastor Mensah and Pastor Anthony I remember fighting and kicking and behaving in a violent manner. After about four hours I was delivered from the spirit that had attacked me.

When I returned home my daughter was in bed very sick. I took her to go to the hospital. The doctor said that she had a very severe form of chickenpox. They had never seen this form in a long time. I had to feed her, bathe her and look after her basic needs. I nearly lost her!

She was soon healed. Her paternal aunt died in Zimbabwe. I phoned to offer my condolences. They told me that she had died of severe chicken pox. Accordingly, the doctors there had not seen such a severe cause before. When this happened I started to think seriously about my life. What was that that could attack my daughter and her aunt simultaneously? I was stunned!

IGNORANCE IS NO DEFENCE

When I came to the ministry I was not planning to stay. My plan was to get healing, deliverance and return back to my usual way of life.

I wanted to use the church for quick fixes for my problems then go my own way. But God had a different plan for me!

While I was going through the deliverance I had a boyfriend with whom I was planning to have a long-term relationship. We never managed to have a physical relationship, each time we tried, something would happen to him or to me and we would stop short of having sex.

Also I was very bitter in my heart, I could not find it in my heart to forgive my ex-husband, I was filing for divorce as I was afraid of his violent temper. I was not sexually active, but sin lingered in my heart each time I planned to do it the subject would be preached in my church. I got very frustrated and was afraid to carry out my plan. Because of my ignorance and bad attitude my deliverance took a long time.

Surely, when I went for the deliverance the devils would be cast out. I could feel them leaving my body. They came out by coughing, sneezing vomiting or yawning or at times I would feel like somebody was cutting me up with a spear or sharp object. All the demons would come out and I would feel good. But when I got home all the demons would return and I could tell when they were back in.

For a whole year I was like that. I call it 'yo-yo' deliverance. I had no peace in my heart and I always felt like running away, where to, I do not know. I began to get desperate. My body was healed but the sex and the eating in the dream would continue and I would continue finding myself in a terrible dilemma.

(Luke 11:24-26) says,
*"When an evil spirit comes out of a man; it goes to arid places seeking for rest and does not find it. Then it says to I will return the house I left. When it arrives it finds the house swept clean and put in order. Then it goes and takes seven other spirits more wickedly than itself; they go in and live there. And the final condition of that man is worse than the first."*

Sometimes I would feel good and other times I would feel so badly that I began to wonder if God really was at work. I blamed everything and everyone including God himself. I could not take responsibility for my sin and attitude. Or to be honest, I was not ready to take a good look at my sinful way of life. Jeremiah says, "The heart is desperately wicked and deceitful, who can know it?" I began to seek God with all my heart. I knew that something was not right with me.

I also began to listen to the teaching of the Archbishop Deya. He is a stickler for Holy living. He lectured on generational curses and why people were cursed.

You know when a man or woman of God speaks on a subject; that the anointing for that subject is always at hand. I made a conscious decision to commit myself fully to the Lord and walk in His Holy ways and to seek Him and serve Him.

In my church we have many services during the day. My bishop believes sincerely in the ministry being open 24hours per day. He says Satan does not rest, we Christians should be vigilant, and trouble does not come only on Sunday mornings only when the doors of the church are open. Trouble can come at any time.

Sometimes we are so overwhelmed that we cannot pray by ourselves but we can always pick up the phone and call the church. Someone is always at the other end of the phone to pray and support us. Also he has policies that if you are very sick and need to call for an ambulance. We need to first call the church. A minister will pray with you on the phone, assess with you whether the sickness is demonic or physical or witchcraft. The issue is then dealt with accordingly. If it's something that warrants going to the hospital then they send you there. Many individuals have gone to have unnecessary treatment at hospitals and have had surgical operations. Only later do they discover that it was witchcraft. Some of the people could be in severe pain but the doctors would send them home because they could not see anything wrong with them.

I have the greatest respect for doctors and nurses. I am one myself. I am not saying that every sickness is demonic. No! I am not saying that you should not go to see your physician when the need arises.

Because of that reason we have many services like at 3 a.m. daily from January to December. We have deliverance services daily at 10 a.m. and at 12 midnight; we also have ministers for emergencies. They are on call to go to the hospitals and homes of the members who are very sick or are having attacks in their homes and as mentioned before in the telephone ministry.

Every Friday, Saturday and Sunday night we have our main services in the evenings at 7 p.m. We also have Sunday morning services at 10 a.m. I began to attend all these services. I began to pay my tithes by Direct Debit. I got rid of all the cursed objects that were in my possession. All the jewellery I had collected over the years went into the dustbin. I got rid of the boyfriend. He was begging me to give him another chance but no I had decided to be rid of him. Jesus would be my boyfriend now.

I began to learn about forgiveness. The hardest thing for me was to forgive my ex- husband. I always remembered clearly everything that he had done to me as if it were yesterday. I used to feel justified to be angry. I would reason that because of him I lost everything. When you say you have forgiven but still think of the incident with pain and bitterness that means you have not really forgiven at all. I would say I forgave with my mouth, but in my heart it was a different matter.

There was a lot of teaching on holding grudges and bitterness but I was so hard-hearted. It took a very long time for the spirit of bitterness and holding grudges to go. Sometimes I would forgive and then got angry and bitter again. It was a vicious cycle.

One day the Lord delivered me from these spirits. I even started to pray for those people who had hurt me. We tried to get back together with my ex-husband but it did not work. He refused counselling and did not want me to worship Jesus so I could not let anything or anybody come between Jesus and me.

God hates divorce and I do not condone it. It has happened to me twice I am not proud of myself. I do not encourage divorce. I am no better than my ex-husband, I just happen to find Jesus first. Now I do not blame my woes on anyone. I am aware that the curses that were in my life caused all the punishment that I received. Satan is a thief. He steals kills and destroys. I can now forgive because I know that I myself have been forgiven.

Also I struggled with pride. At first I was of the opinion that I was humble but God knew otherwise. The Jezebel spirit was also cast out of me. Each time this spirit was cast out I would scream and manifest heavily. By nature I was used to getting my own way. They call it being ambitious and strong-willed. On any given day I would get my own way. I would manipulate by: sulking, lying, complaining, threats, position, shame, pity, And confrontations,

## UNBELIEF

Because of my profession as a nurse I found it very hard to believe that the healings - especially of incurable diseases - actually cured had taken place. So I had the spirit of unbelief and I was a sceptic. I have learnt how disease strikes and kills individuals so I found it very hard to believe the testimonies of the people who were healed. I needed to know how it happened - I had to have a scientific or medical explanation.

I have seen many miracles in the church in which I worship. Up until God healed me of anorexia nervosa, Crohn's disease, anaemia, palpitations, fatigue, etc. I found it hard to believe in these miraculous manifestations of the Holy Spirit.

This spirit of unbelief is present in many churches and the people do not grow in the Lord even if they witness God's handiwork in people's lives. It took me about two years to believe in God's miraculous healing powers.

When I started being delivered I was very reluctant to pray. I believed that if the ministers prayed for me then I did not have to pray for myself. Yes, their prayers were powerful and working, but I also needed to adopt an active prayer life too. We need to be active in resisting the Devil from entering our lives.

My archbishop is an expert in the knowledge of generational curses. Through his teaching I began to fully understand the various curses that had befallen my life and my family. I started to confess and repent of my sins. I named the sins one by one. I was not ashamed to repent of the terrible sins I had committed.

I began to understand why I behaved in the way that I did and why I never grew much in the Lord. I suggest you read these books by Gilbert Deya "The Stronghold of Generational Curses" and "The Curses of Sexual Sins." I started to repent for the sins of myself, my family, children, forefathers etc. Generally life improved. The curses of poverty, singleness, sickness, barren-ness etc. were broken.

Witchcraft spells that were placed on me were playing havoc with my life. Jealousy and hatred were making me ill. The Lord in His mercy delivered me from all this! The things that I have discussed already were hindering my deliverance. I began to get deliverance and to receive Christian revelation.

I have a Brazilian friend Marina Huss. She encouraged me to read books on deliverance written by a doctor called Rebecca Brown on deliverance. I bought these books and I began to gain spiritual insight. Reading these books made me understand why I was going through the problems which I did. I began to experience deliverance and gain spiritual insights.

I began to hate sin and my motives started to change. Initially I had come for a quick fix to my problems; I just wanted to use the church as a supermarket. Pick up my healing, and then go on my way. But I began to meet and know Jesus. I fell in love with him. Now I love God for who He is, not what He can do for me?

## DIVINE DELIVERNCE IN INDIA

I became an usher in the church. I immersed myself with God's business. I left my job as a nurse to concentrate on the work of God and on my deliverance. I used to travel with my bishop and other ministers all over the world for crusades and ministry. Each time I went on a crusade I experienced a big breakthrough. I never used to pray or ask for these things. The Lord allowed them happen.

First I went to Brazil when I worked very hard and thoroughly enjoyed myself in that crusade. When I returned to England I witnessed a financial breakthrough. I moved from a very expensive property to a similar type of house where the mortgage was less.

Another time I went to Bangalore in India. In that crusade I was very much troubled by demonic spirits. Four of us had travelled together: Bishop, Pastor Ron, Jeanette and I. along with the rest ahead of us.

As we were in transit in Dubai we had lunch. After lunch I was getting more and more upset with my archbishop. I asked him why I was still suffering from demonic torment and sickness. I reminded him that it was now two and a half years since I was supposed to be delivered and I was still experiencing the problems. Why was it that I was still manifesting I asked him. I was so tired of the devils in me. He just looked at me and did not say anything in response to my queries. He had a lot of emphathy for me and my issues

When we arrived in India it seemed as if the whole world was against me. I just wanted to cry. I refused to speak to anybody or have anything to do with anyone. The only person whom I could cope with was Jean-Jeanette. She was very patient with me as she had gone through deliverance herself and understood my problems. To make matters worse, my feet were swollen from the long flight and my head was pounding. I just wanted to sleep.

I had little sleep that day and I had to go to the crusade grounds. On the first day of that crusade I beheld wonderful success. I saw the eyes of the blind opened, the deaf regained their hearing, the sick were healed and my swollen legs became whole again and my headache went away.

We returned to our hotel and stayed up with Jeanette in our room. We were discussing why I became so tired and why I was still being possessed with demons. She suggested that we pray all night and present our requests to God. We presented our petitions to God. My petition to God was, "Please Lord, do not let me go back to London still being possessed with demons." I wanted complete deliverance in India. I was tired of being slapped about by unseen hands. I wanted to be a free woman. I needed to have peace in my life. I had never known true peace before.

So we prayed together all night and in faith, believing that God was able to do what He said He would do. By the time we finished it was 5 a.m. we then went to sleep. I was so tired that I slept throughout the day. I noticed that that night was free from demonic dreams.

Then the full schedule of the crusade started. We went to the Crusade grounds. As soon as the Archbishop started speaking, I was manifesting.

I do not remember much, but my colleagues told me that I was vomiting a lot of blood. The Indian people also were being delivered. The anointing of deliverance and healing was very strong on that trip in Bangalore. I was vomiting so much blood caused by curses that had been given to me by witchcraft and the blood covenants which involved killing chickens and other animals. By the time I woke up the meeting was over. I saw and heard nothing. Jeanette helped me to clean up. Then we returned to the hotel. We did the same again. We prayed all night and we went to bed in the morning.

# CHAPTER 11

## THE ANGEL MICHAEL

ANGELIC VISITATION

After I went to my bed I saw in a vision or dream a nice man approach me. He said that his name was Michael and he had come from the throne of God. He said he was going to operate on me and remove all the dirt that was in my stomach. He laid me down on a theatre table and performed a laparotomy on my stomach. He scooped lots of blood from my inside. Metallic objects were also coming out of me - some of the metal was gold and it was pure. Also some strange children were coming out of me. I could feel the pulling and tugging of my inside but I felt no pain. Also I could not wake up. He sewed me up, and gave me a thorough cleaning. When I woke up the following day I knew something had happened to my belly. I ran to the mirror to check my stomach to see if there were any stitches there. There was none. I looked normal. There was no cut or mark on me. I did not know the significance of this, so I kept it to myself. I rested a lot during the day. In the evening we went to the crusade grounds again. My friends were urging me to carry a plastic bag in case I started to vomit. I took their advice.

As soon as the ministration started, I also started vomiting lots of blood clots again. I was crying a lot. Apparently the same thing that was happening to me was happening to the crowd. I was so shocked when I saw the video of the crusade in India. I was there manifesting with the Indians. The anointing for deliverance and healing was mighty. I only woke up after the ministration was finished.

We returned to the hotel and we did the same thing again. We prayed all night but this time, two other friends from London - Emma and Vivian joined us. When I went to bed another vision happened to me. The same man returned. He told me that he was going to operate on me again.

He sat me in a dentist chair. And took the bottom set of my teeth out of my mouth and put it on the side. He then put his foot on my jaw and used a sharp instrument like the one that dentists use to extract teeth. He extracted certain things from my gums. I do not know what they were up to that time. Blood was gushing out of my mouth but I was not afraid.

When he finished, he cleaned me up and put my bottom teeth back in my mouth. I woke up in the morning knowing that somebody had touched my mouth. When I went to look at my mouth in the mirror all my teeth were there and they all looked normal.

I still did not understand it but I kept it all to myself. Now I believe he was taking out the demons of talking too much. I used to talk nonsense. You know some women talk until they drive their husbands crazy. I was like that. I could drive people crazy by my non-stop talking. I could talk for England

Each time I went to the crusade grounds the same thing happened to me. We went to the crusade grounds. We had heavy deliverance. Then we returned to the hotel, prayed all night and went to bed.

This time the man came back again and he said he was going to operate on my head. He put me in a special position as when someone is having brain surgery. This time he cut the back of my skull. He flipped my cranium over and began to scoop things from my brain. Lots of stuff came out and he cleaned me up. He put the skull back on my head and left. The same thing happened again and I woke up wandering what was happening to me. I could not tell anyone because I thought they would not believe me. I did not even understand it myself. I woke up feeling much better. I was in a good mood and was relating to the others better. I felt a big difference in my body. I was so exhausted by all this that I used to stay in my hotel room in the afternoons to get extra rest.

One afternoon I was lying in bed in my room, and was looking away from the window. Then something strange happened to me. I saw outside the window a red monkey and a big red snake coiled outside the tree that was outside my window. Remember I was facing away from the window. So this could only have been a vision. The two were looking very sad and they wanted me to feel sorry for them. They said to me, "Please Mabel, let us back in, we have lived in you since you were born. We have nowhere else to go." I said, "No. Go away in Jesus name." They disappeared. This made me realise that for the demons to enter you, you have to give them permission. Remember also how satan entered Judas Iscariot

Also if you go through heavy deliverance and nothing happens, then.   It is important to pray as in the example that Jesus gave to the disciples in (Mark 9:28-29).
*After Jesus had gone indoors, his disciples asked him privately, "Why could we not drive it out?" He then replied, "This kind can come out only by prayer."*

By the time the meetings had finished I only remember the first day and the last day of the crusade. The rest Jesus knows.

When we returned home to England we were upgraded on the plane to first class. Because of that my feet did not swell when I arrived home. I remember arriving in my house on a Tuesday afternoon. I only managed to stay in my lounge. I slept for three days. I could not eat or drink anything. I only managed to go to the bathroom and back to bed. As I slept I felt as if it was on fire.

At one point I woke up to see in my room an unnatural bright white. My bed felt like I was sleeping on feathers the feeling was so ecstatic that I thought I was in heaven. I just said to God, "Lord I know it is you. I know that you are here." I went back to sleep.

I can compare this to (Psalms 91:4),
> *"He will cover you with his feathers and under his wings you will find refuge, His faithfulness will be your shield and rampart."*

From that time onwards the bad dreams disappeared. Sex and eating in the dream also disappeared. Hatred for men went out the window. The demonic talkativeness went and my whole attitude changed. Indeed I am a new creation. God has really renewed my mind!

## THE EXPLANATION OF WHAT HAPPENED IN INDIA

When I went to church the following week my archbishop called the people who had gone to India with him to give our testimonies. I was saying to myself I do not know what to say, as I do no recall much of what happened at the meetings. I asked if I could speak first so that the others who had a lot to say would speak for a longer period. When I narrated what had happened to me in India the archbishop said to me that that was divine deliverance. He said that I had had angelic visitation. He began to tell me that that I was going to be a powerful deliverance minister. And that he could see the glory of God upon me as I walked in church that Saturday. After all those years of pain, confusion, curses, ignorance and waste, the Lord finally delivered me!

(Obadiah 17) says,
*"But upon mount Zion shall be deliverance, and there shall be holiness, and the house of Jacob shall possess their possessions.*

*Now I have a very strong desire to see people getting delivered, healed and set free. I love to see born again children of God walking in their full potential. It is very important to walk in knowledge.*

*(Hosea 4:6). My people are destroyed from lack of knowledge. Because you have rejected knowledge I also reject you as my priests, because you have ignored the law of your God I will also ignore your children."*

# CHAPTER 12

## NOT THIS TIME DEVIL

## DOORWAYS THAT LED TO MY DEMONIC MANIFESTATIONS

God protects people so that devils cannot violate them or enter them. This goes for both Christians and non-Christians. God never allows devils the free choice which human beings possess. The only way the devil can enter a human being is when an opening is made. This is like a break in the protection of God. Sin breaks a hole in the protective hedge, many times allowing a devil to really enter into the person committing the sin. This point of entry is called a doorway. They are different doorways through which devils can enter a person. I will discuss with you how I became to be demonised and cursed.

## INHERITANCE

From the days of fleeing Chaka Zulu to the time I was born, no one in my family knew Jehovah God. They only knew about the ancestral spirits which our forefathers worshipped. They pass this knowledge from generation to generation. Most of my family laughed and mocked Christians. So in my generation there is a long list of forefathers who did not acknowledge Jehovah Yahweh. (Exodus 34:6-7) says that, "And he passed in front of Moses, Proclaiming the Lord, the compassionate and gracious God, slow to anger and abounding in love and faithfulness, maintaining love to thousands and forgiving wickedness, rebellion and sin. Yet he does not leave the guilty unpunished, he punishes the children and their children for the sin of the fathers to the third and fourth generation."

Without a doubt the sins of my ancestors had a profound effect on my spiritual well being. I am now aware why certain things happened to me. I was not given any instruction about Jesus Christ or about Christianity. I was burdened by the curses of my ancestors. Added to this I indulged in a sinful way of life. I only knew ancestral worship and masquerade dancing. I was cognisant only of ancestor worship and masquerade dancing.

(Psalm 51:5) says
*"Surely I was sinful at birth, sinful from the time my mother conceived me."*

Obviously my grandparents took oaths to the demonic gods they served. These rituals were done in secret. My dad used to insist all along that he would never serve any other gods but the gods of his ancestors. These oaths are binding upon the lives of their offspring. In my case, as a descendant of these people I was bound whether I knew it or not.

Until a few years ago I had no idea that this would be a problem in my life. In a way it is good that my grandparents told me about their heritage and culture. I was able to pinpoint exactly what were the origins of these problems.

I also encourage those who have parents who are members of Lodges, Freemasons, The Mormon Church and members of other cults and religions that do not see Jesus as the only way to God, to come to the living God through Christ. If you really want to be set free, Jesus is able to do so. We also have the Holy Spirit who is able to search all things and to tell us all the things we do not know about.

SOLUTION

If you suspect that you were dedicated to Satan or his demons from in your youth, it is important to confess the sins of your forefathers, and ask the Lord Jesus to forgive and cleanse you from these sins. Let Jesus cleanse you from the iniquities of your forefathers. Renounce aloud any dedication placed upon your life; proclaim that you are now in the Lord Jesus Christ and for His service only. Then in the name of

Jesus Christ cast out the demons that were placed in your life. Take authority in the name of Jesus Christ over the curse of destruction that was activated through the broken dedication, and command it to be broken immediately in the name of Jesus. Also in His name command all the devils associated with that curse to leave you at once. Now the blood of Jesus is the most powerful tool we have at our disposal. Always plead the blood of Jesus.

I find the prayer of (Daniel 9) very powerful in dealing with generational and inherited curses. Starting from (verse 4) it says,

*"I prayed to the Lord my God and confessed; O Lord the great and awesome God, who keeps his covenant of love with all who love him and obey his commands, we have sinned an done wrong. We have been wicked and have rebelled; we have turned away from your commands, and laws. We have not listened to your servants the prophets, who spoke in your name to our kings, our princes and our fathers, and to all people of the land. Lord you are righteous, but this day we are covered with shame- the men of Judah and the people of Jerusalem and all Israel, both near and far, in all the countries were you have scattered us because of our unfaithfulness to you. O Lord, our kings, and we our princes our fathers are covered with shame because we have sinned against you. The Lord our God is merciful and forgiving, even though we have rebelled against him and we have not obeyed the Lord our God or kept the laws he gave us through his servants the prophets. All Israel has transgressed your law and turned away, refusing to obey you. Therefore the curses and sworn judgement written in the Law of Moses, the servant of God, have been poured out on us, because we have sinned against you. You have fulfilled the words spoken against us and against our rulers by bringing upon us a great disaster. Under the whole heaven nothing has ever been done like what has been done to Jerusalem.*

*Just as it is written in the Law of Moses, all this disaster has come upon us, yet we have not sought favour of the Lord our God by turning away from our sins and giving attention to your truth. The Lord did not hesitate to bring the disaster upon us, for the Lord our God is righteous in everything he does; yet we have not obeyed him.*

*Now O Lord our God who brought your people out of Egypt with a mighty hand and who made for yourself a name that endures for this day, we have sinned, we have done wrong. O Lord in keeping with your righteous acts, turn away your anger and your wrath from Jerusalem, your city and your holy hill. Our sins and the iniquities of our fathers have made Jerusalem and your people an object of scorn to all those around us. Now our God hear the prayers hear the prayers and petitions of your servants of your servant. For your sake, O Lord, look with favour on your desolate sanctuary. Give ear O God and hear; open your eyes and see the desolation of the city that bears your Name. We do not make request of you because we are righteous, but because of your great mercy. O Lord listens! O Lord forgives! O Lord hears and acts. For your sake, O my God, does not delay, because your city and your people bear your Name."*

While I was speaking and praying, confessing my sin and the sin of my people Israel and making my request to the Lord my God for his holy hill- while I was still in prayer, Gabriel, the man I had seen in the earlier vision, came to me in swift flight about the time of the evening sacrifice. He instructed me and said to me, Daniel I have now come to give you insight and understanding.

As soon as you began to pray, an answer was given which I have come to give you, for you are highly esteemed. Therefore consider the message and understand the vision. Seventy sevens are decreed for your people and your Holy city to finish transgression, to put an end to sin, to atone for wickedness, to bring everlasting righteousness, to seal up vision and prophecy and to anoint the most holy.

It looks like for every sin and curse there is a time that God sets for atonement but now we have the Lord Jesus and His Word says that those who call on the name of the Lord shall be delivered (Joel 2: 32). SEX

Someone whom I knew and trusted once raped me. I could not share this secret with anybody for at least twenty years. I could not report to the police because I was a minor and I was afraid to tell my parents, as they had warned me before, not to get involved with a person like him. I hated men for that reason I loathed men who hide under a jacket of respectability and yet deep down they are rapists and abusers of children.

Some of the rapists and child molesters go to church and even hold positions of authority. This resulted in some of the strongest demons being put in me because of the trauma and the violence that came with it: Hatred of men, hatred of self, bitterness, fear, rejection, anger, - worthlessness and inferiority complex – all these were the result.

I became very rude, loud and talkative as a way of protecting myself. Later on I used to watch blue movies. That also helped to entertain more demonic influences in my life.

Generally speaking, sex before marriage brings curses in people's lives. The same goes for homosexuality, fornication, masturbation, perversion, incest and adultery.

(1 CORINTHIANS 6:18-20) says
*"Flee from sexual immorality. All other sins a man commits are outside his body but he who sins sexually sins against his own. Do you not know that your body is the temple of the Holy Spirit, who is in you, whom you have received from God? You are not your own you were bought at a price. Therefore honour God with your body."*

The Biblical King David was punished very severely because of the immoral sex he had with Bathsheba. He ended up murdering an innocent man. This resulted in his household being cursed. Read (2nd Samuel Chapters 11 and 12). After this came incidents of rape and incest in his household. Absalom conspired against him, and David had to flee Jerusalem for a while. He lost the respect of his subjects when he was fleeing from Absalom; Shimei had the courage to curse him even though he was a king. Death of children frequently occurred in his home.

Rebellion also started in his kingdom, When Shimei rebelled against David in 2 Samuel chapters 20. From the day David did that to the day he died he had a lot of problems with his children. The prophet Nathan told King David off, in no uncertain terms that he should repent (Psalm 51). Even after repentance he still had to pay for the consequences of his sin. What has your dad done that you can be punished for? The Bible says that our forefathers have sinned and they are not around to take the punishment. Therefore somebody has to take that punishment you could be that third and fourth generation even though you may be true in from generations moved.

SOLUTION

Abstain from sexual immorality. If you were already involved, proclaim and renounce every unclean activity in which you have ever been involved. Then verbally forgive everyone who violated you, including the person or persons who raped you or molested you in childhood. Forgiving these individuals does not mean you agree with what they did to you, but it means that through the forgiveness you can secret the ties that that can keep you channel to the injury they brought to your life. I suggest that women counsel women and men counselling men. The demons of sex are very strong and cunning. By counselling the opposite sex, temptation might arise. We know the plans of the enemy. A lot of ministers have been caught up in this way. We are aware of Satan's tactics. Deliverance may take time, but the child of God should persevere. Soon the God of peace will crush Satan under our feet (Romans 16:20).

GOING TO THE WITCHDOCTORS (OBEAH MEN)

I grew up in a witchdoctor's house. My granddad was a well-known witch doctor. Most Africans now understand where I am coming from.

When my Nan died my aunt took my brother and I to a witchdoctor to find out the cause of her death. We were quite young so we did what ever my aunt suggested. When we got to the witchdoctor's place we listened to what my aunt and the witchdoctor were discussing. My aunt was told that it was my other aunt who had killed my Nan, by means of witchcraft.

The witchdoctor then cut us with a razor blade and put some portions on the bleeding cuts. This was meant to protect us from the other aunt's witchcraft. We began to fear and hate my other aunt, because the witchdoctor informed us that she was the witch that had killed Nan. Whether this was true or not I don't know but most of my relatives take what the witchdoctor says as gospel truth.

My second visit to the witchdoctor's was with my first husband. I had given birth by caesarean section; they did not like it at all. Automatically witchcraft was said to be the culprit. The witchdoctor said my womb was tied by the witchcraft. He wanted me to bring a white chicken to offer to the ancestors so that my womb would be released. He put his hand on my belly button and removed something from it. He showed all who were there what had been extracted from my womb. I saw the object with my own eyes so I believed what he was saying. From that time until I started going for deliverance I never experienced my period. I went into premature menopause. I went for a different issue I came back with pre mature menopause and bareness

I remember when I was going through deliverance I used to feel certain things coming out of my private parts. I was in violation of the word of God by seeking the help of the witchdoctors. In (Lev 19:31) the Word of God clearly states not to turn to mediums or seek out spirits, for you will be defiled by them. "I am the Lord your God."

SOLUTION

It is always important to confess our faith in the Lord Jesus Christ. In this way He can always intervene for us. Then confess all the sins of consulting witchdoctors, or any visit to anyone God does not approve of.

(1 John 1:9) says,
*"God is faithful because he has promised. He is just because Jesus has already paid the penalty for our sins."*

Be honest about the sin and acknowledge the sin it is.

In my case it was the visits to the witchdoctor. After confession and repenting of all the sins, confession alone is not enough.

(Proverbs 28:13) says,
*"He who covers his sins will not prosper; but whoever confesses and forsakes them will have mercy."*

NEVER EVER GO TO CONSULT THE WITCHDOCTOR AGAIN.

Get rid of all the things the witchdoctor gave you to use. A book, charms, objects of art etc. because it is now an abomination in the sight of God. In our church the pastor encourages you to bring those objects to the church and then burn them. Take your stand with God. If you do not have enough faith then go to a church where they minister deliverance.


OCCULTIC DOORWAYS

No matter how lightly or heavily we deal with the occult it will be a snare to you. A good friend of mine read my palms then he gave me a lot of advice – which I have now renounced. I also used to read my horoscope on a regular basis. I am aware that fortune telling, reading books on the occult, Ouija boards, meditation of any kind which is not the word of God, magic and tealeaf readers are not merely harmless fun.

It might look like that but it opens a doorway for demonic entrance. It is a contradiction to the word of God in (Deuteronomy 18:10-12) which says, "Let no one be found among you who sacrifices his sons or daughters in the fire, who practices divination or sorcery, interprets omens, engages in witchcraft or casts spells, or who is a medium or spiritist or who consults the dead. Anyone who does these things is detestable to the Lord and because of these detestable practices the Lord your God will drive out those nations before you. You must blameless before the Lord."

SOLUTION

Pray:

"I confess my involvement in the occult. I recognised that such a thing is an abomination to you and detestable in your sight, I humbly ask you to forgive me my sin in getting involved with the occult. I ask you to lift up any demonic entrance as a result of my actions and to cleanse me from my sins and to close that doorway forever with the precious blood of Jesus. I ask in the name of my Lord and saviour Jesus Christ.
Amen.

Speak to Satan out loud and say, "You Satan and your demons I have asked my God for forgiveness for my involvement with the occult and I Am forgiven. I now close that doorway to you forever through the blood of Jesus. I command you to leave in the name of Jesus and never come back."

DRUNKENESS

Drinking alcohol was very normal in my family. That was our way of relaxing. My mum and dad, my uncles and aunts, they all drank. To be drunk was no big deal. Children got offered sips of alcohol here and there. They got used to drink at an early age.

I used to drink to drown my sorrows. I would drink until I passed out. The bottle was a way of escaping reality, or rather, not wanting to face my problems. When drunk I used to hallucinate and see various images. Now I understand that these images were scenes from the demonic realm.

This is the means by which demons enter these who abuse drugs. They get addicted and they get their highs and lows, which are produced by these drugs. After my divorce I stopped drinking because I had to drive. Even though I had stopped, the alcohol had already done its damage.

SOLUTION

PRAY AS IN THE ABOVE PRAYER. CONFESS, REPENT, RENOUNCE AND CAST OUT DEMONS IN THE NAME OF JESUS.

DEMONIC LUST

A long time after I had my divorce I went through a most terrible experience with the spirit of lust. I tried with all my strength to fight it. My mind knew very well from what I was being taught in church that I should not fornicate, but my body was saying something else. This used to torment me so much.

That is why we have many who commit fornication and adultery are even in the church. Individuals can be very sincere in their walk with Christ, but their body is pulling them in another direction. This is rarely spoken about in the church. I struggled with that and because of the shame I was feeling I could not confide in anyone. I used to pray prayers like "God please kill my feelings". But the more I prayed the worse it got. One day the urge was so strong in me that I knew I had to do something, these urges were either going to stop that day or I was going to fornicate. So I did a dramatic thing. I walked in my archbishop's office.

It was a glass walled office so we always saw what he was up to even though we did not hear him.

I begged him not to look at me until I said what I needed to say. I confided in him what I was going through; he did not look at me so I felt comfortable speaking to him. He just said to me, "Daughter, go on your way you will never feel like that again." True to the Man of God's word, my lust subsided. God was able to keep my body holy until the day I got remarried. Still because I had committed that sin in my thoughts, I had to repent and close that doorway to the Devil.

So I had found this law at work - when I wanted to do good, evil was right there with me. For in my inner being I delighted in God's law, but I see another law at work in the members of my body, waging war against the law of my mind and making me a prisoner of the law of sin within my body. What a wretched man I am! Who will rescue from this body of death? Thanks be to God – through Jesus Christ our lord! So then I myself in my mind am a slave to God's law, but in the sinful nature a slave to the law of sin. (Romans 7:21-25.)

## LAYING OF HANDS

I am very sensitive about who I submit myself to lay hands on me. Laying on of hands can be a powerful spiritual experience, a temporal interaction between two opposing forces, through which supernatural power is released. Power flows from one person to another. This power can be good or evil. It can come from the Holy Spirit of God, or from satanic forces. Because I wanted a quick fix to my problems I submitted myself to anybody whom I thought could help me. I went to a white garment church in Zimbabwe and they laid hands on me. From what I have learnt now that church is from the sea. They gave me water and salt to sprinkle in my house to ward off evil spirits. I went to different churches and had any Tom, Dick and Harry lay their hands on me.

I was ignorant of the fact that witches come to church too. They lay their hands on Christians and they transfer demons into them. As a minister now, I do not lay hands on anyone just like that. The word of God says not to lay hands suddenly. I need to be acquainted with what I am dealing with. When I am not right with God I do not lay hands on anyone. I also respect people's desires not to be touched. I encourage all children of God to test every spirit.

## IDLE WORDS

Every time I became distraught I would ask God to take my life. A few times I even tried to commit suicide.

One time I was speaking to pastor Baka and said something like, "Please God, kill me." He quickly chided me for uttering these words and rebuked the statement I had just made. He gave me a Psalm to meditate on (Psalm 118:17) which says "I shall not die but I shall live to declare the works of the Lord."

He made me realise that we have to be careful of every word that comes out of our mouth. He said to me that when I speak like that, the demons of death and destruction are activated in my life. They rise up to cause literal death in the life of anyone who speaks thus. He reminded me that death and life are in the tongue. The Spirit of Death and destruction kept tormenting me because I kept inviting it into my life because of ignorance.

Some parents use bad language in front of their children. When the children grow they turn up to be just as bad as their parents. Jesus warned us about the idle words we speak in (Matthew 12:36-37) "But I tell you, men will give account on the day of judgement for every careless word they have spoken. For by your words you will be acquitted and by your words you will be condemned."

## NAMES

I was named after my Nan on my paternal side. Unbeknownst to me, the name brought me soul ties that now bonded me with her even after she died. She died in 1986. When I was going through deliverance in 2001 a demon masquerading as her was wailing and begging to stay in me. Now my Nan is definitely dead. Her soul is either in heaven or hell that I do not know. Some individuals in my culture like to deal with the dead. They believe that the dead can help them. They are happy and see it as a blessing when they see their dead relations in the dream. It is not your relatives you are seeing. It is demons masquerading as your dead relatives deceiving you. Each time I dreamt of the dead I learnt to take authority over that bad dream. I cancelled it with the blood of Jesus.

## SOUL TIES

(EZEKIEL13:18- 22)
*"This is what the sovereign lord says: Woe to the women who sew magic charms on all their wrists and make veils of various length for their heads in order to ensnare people. Will you ensnare the lives of my people but preserve the lives of your own? You have profaned me among my people for a few handfuls of barley and scraps of bread. By lying to my people, who listen to lies, you have killed those who should not have died and spared those who should not live."*

*Hence this is what the Sovereign Lord says. "I am against your magic charms with which you ensnare people like birds and I will tear them from your arms. I will set free the people you ensnare like birds. I will tear off your veils and save my people from your hands, and they will no longer fall prey to your power. Then you will know that I am the Lord. Because you disheartened the righteous with your lies, when I had brought them no grief, and because you encouraged the wicked not to turn from their evil ways and so save their lives therefore you will no longer see false visions and practice divination. I will save my people from your hands. And then you will know that I am the Lord."*

My soul was united together with my ex-lovers with negative repercussions consequences. I went on to my next relationship without severing all soul ties with my previous partners. I had domineering aunts who were very manipulative. Witchcraft also created heavy negative soul ties. My soul was fragmented and destroyed. I never felt whole or complete. Something was always missing in me and I did not know what it was.

I never had peace I could never settle in one place for too long. I could never keep a job for any length of time. I felt that somebody was calling my name and I could not see them. Something was always tugging me away from them. During the deliverance the minister was breaking every soul tie, every spirit tie and every evil cords. We were advised to pray and ask God to send His angels to recover the fragments of my soul and put them back in order, by the order of the Holy Spirit. The Lord did so. He restored and healed my soul. He broke off all bonds to evil spirits and to evil demons. Now I am prisoner to no one – no spirit, no demon, not even to the Devil himself now I feel whole and more settled.


## HOPELESSNESS

My ex- husband always called me fat and ugly. He criticized everything I did. According to him I did nothing good. He continually belittled me. I ended up feeling fat and ugly even though I am a very small woman. My self-esteem was very low. If you see me in real life I am a very small person. How did I feel so fat? I do not even understand how I believed such lies. That is one of the reasons that led to my obsession with food. Now food does not control me. Only Jesus was able to restore me.


## CURSE PINS

Most African people routinely have themselves cut by razor blades. They use: potions, metal, bones, teeth, rock, snake skins and other fetishes that are rubbed into cuts made on their bodies.

I was no exception. I was cut and different herbs and concoctions rubbed into my skin. I thought that that was beneficial to me. My Nan had lots of these cuts I asked her why hers were so big she told me that it was for cosmetic reasons. In her day as a youth you had to have it done to be considered beautiful and eligible for marriage. Most Africans are aware of the reasons for these practices. Your parents and elders tell you that it is good for you and that is for your protection, for good luck and to fend off evil, or some other such reason.

You believe and go along with that practice. I was no exception. I voluntarily, had myself cut. Sometimes I would wake up with cuts in my body. That would have happened during the night. We all knew that that was witchcraft at work.

Like I said I used to read books on deliverance. I discovered that the reason they insert pins into dolls was for the purpose of destroying the person under your control. If you notice how it is, any one of you who has been to the witchdoctors for one reason or the other, they solve one problem, but you end up with other problems, sometimes worse than the ones before.

That proves to me that Satan can heal. I call it demonic healing. But, it comes at a price. Anyway, once a person has these things done to her, it does not matter where she goes, the witches and demons will always find and torment that person. When the person turns to Jesus Christ the demons that came in at the time of the insertion of the pins will rise up to try and bring about the physical death of the person. For that reason I always had suicide in mind. My cuts were small and many. There were some I did not know about. Some people say that when they woke up in the morning they had these cuts on their bodies. They have the understanding of what these cuts were for. Instead of seeking the Lord's help they sought help from witchdoctors.

In many African and middle eastern countries men get circumcised. Women have that done to them in certain African cultures. Not in mine. If you have been circumcised in your culture, the knife could be demonic. They do it by the power of witchcraft. In some tribes that I know of if you do not get circumcised as a boy and they find out that, they will come to get you. The elders of that tribe make a beeline for your residence. Usually the man cannot flee because he will be paralysed by the power of witchcraft and he gets circumcised by hook or by crook.

- 151 -

In some tribes women are forced to be circumcised. What strikes me with horror is that it is done by other women. They put a lot of herbs and concoctions after the circumcision. This usually results in septicaemia and the victim dies. One of my good friends was circumcised as a child. That has caused her to have lots of gynaecological problems. Her menstrual flow is very abnormal. She has had to go to the doctors to have her canal enlarged so that her menstruation could be eased. She vows that she will never send her children back to Africa as she fears for their safety. She believes what they did to her might be done to her daughters as well.

## HOW I DEALT WITH THE CURSE PINS

I was thoroughly disgusted with myself when I found out what had been done to me. I personally had volunteered to have this procedure done to me. When I realized what I had done, I did not wait to go to the deliverance room. I knelt down in my bedroom and I confessed and repented of my sins of having myself cut like that. I anointed my whole body with olive oil. Then I prayed out loudly. "Lord Jesus, here I come again you know what I let myself into. I got cut and I encouraged it. I am asking you in your mercy to flow your Holy Spirit into my body and do whatever is necessary to remove all the curse pins in my body. Please remove completely all the demons that came with these curse pins."

I could not go any further because I felt a terrible sharp cutting pain all over my body. I was screaming and crying for what seemed to be for ages. After the pain had subsided I went to look at myself in the mirror, my body was red and inflamed. It took a whole week for the redness and inflammation to go away.

## PERSONAL ITEMS

When I was growing up I remember that many mornings I would wake up to find a big chunk of hair missing from my head. Many people in the neighbourhood had these complaints. This was always neatly done and I never felt anything in my sleep. Some people say that they dreamt of someone cutting their hair with a pair scissors. My parents and aunts would dismiss it as nothing inconsequential.

Also over the years I have had items of clothing, especially underwear and photographs go missing. It is a known factor that friends, relation's witches can take these items to the witchdoctors to put a curse on the owner of these possessions. The demon spirits need these items to identify the person they are being sent to destroy.

Some of these things happened to me many years ago so I cannot retrieve these objects now. But God being a powerful God has made provision for our deliverance. So I prayed and asked God to destroy the stolen articles and render them powerless for demonic use. I then commanded all the curses to be broken and the demons associated with curses to come out forever.

I am now very sensitive about which hairdresser I go to the same with the manicurists and beauty therapists. Some of them are there to collect from Christians, hair, nails and other things for the purpose of destroying the lives of individuals.


## WRONG CHOICES/ FOOLISH CHOICES OR WICKED CHOICES

I made many wrong choices; no one forced me to make these choices. I had free will. But I made some bad choices, some of which affected me adversely. Guess whom I blamed for my wrong choices - God!

In (Ruth 1) it says,
*"In the days when Judges ruled, there was famine in the land, and a man from Bethlehem in Judah, together with his wife and two sons went to live for a while in the country of Moab. The man's name was Elimelech, his wife's name, Naomi, and the names of the two*

- 153 -

*sons were Mahlon and Kilion. They were Ephrathites from*
*Bethlehem in Judah. And they went to Moab and Lived there,*
*Now Elimelech, Naomi's husband died and she was left with her*
*two sons. They married Moabite women, one named Orpah and the*
*other Ruth. After they lived there for about ten years, both Mahlon*
*and Chilion also died and Naomi was left without her two sons and*
*her husband.*
*When she heard in Moab that the Lord had come to the aid of his*
*people by providing food for them, Naomi and her daughters in law*
*prepared to return home from therewith her two daughters in law she*
*left the place were she had been living and set out on the road that*
*would take them back to the land Judah."*

See what happens here, because of hunger a man left a blessed people to go and live among a Godless people. He probably joined in their pagan worship. The Moabites are cursed by God and so is their land. They were not allowed to come to the temple of the Lord.

When he got there he found death, the grave was waiting for him because he had violated the Lord's law. Later on, his sons married the women who were cursed and they also died. Naomi was left with no husband and no sons. (Verse 8) says "then Naomi said to her two daughters-in-law, go back each of you to your mother's home. May the Lord Show kindness to you as you have shown to the dead and to me? May the Lord grant that each of you will find rest in the home of another husband?"

Then she kissed them and they wept aloud and said to her. "We will go back with you to your people." But Naomi said, "Return home, my daughters, why would you come with me? Am I going to have any more sons who could become your husbands? Return home my daughters; I am too old to have another husband. Even if I thought there was still hope for me- even if I had a husband tonight and then give birth to sons, would you wait until they grew up? Would you remain unmarried for them? No my daughters. It is more bitter for me than for you, because the Lord's hand has gone out against me!" At this they wept again.

Now see the choices each of the daughters in law made.

Then Orpah kissed her mother-in-law good-bye but Ruth clung to her. Look said Naomi; "your sister in law is going back to her people and to her gods. Go back with her." But Ruth replied. "Don't urge me to leave you or turn back from you. Where you go I will go, and were you stayed I will stay. Your people will be my people and your God my God. Where you die I will die and there I will be buried. May the Lord deal with me be it ever so severely, if anything but death separates you and me."

When Naomi realised that Ruth was determined to go with her, she stopped urging her to leave.

From what we know after that incident, a Moabites woman was allowed into the Israelite camp. She became the great-great-grandmother of our Lord Jesus Christ. Make the right choice and things will go well with you. By the same token, if you make the wrong choice then the consequences would be disastrous. Some of the things that happen to people are as a direct result of the choices that they made at some previous point in this life.

## HOW I MET MY HUSBAND

After going through that torment and getting set free from all that was harassing my life, I began to long to get remarried. I now adopted a healthy attitude towards men. I decided to spend much of my time in the house of God.

Time came to go to Kenya for a miracle crusade. A team from London including myself went. I had an exhilarating feeling during this crusade. This was the first time I was going to a crusade demon free. We saw people being set free from all sorts of bondages. The meetings were that Spirit-filled!

During the weekends we were sent to different churches. We went in twos and threes. I went with my very good friend Vivian Taiwan. We were allocated a village in Kisumu called Kibosi. I will never forget the experience we had there. On our way to the village our car broke down. We had to get out of the car and push it. By the time we arrived at the meeting it was late and the congregation had been waiting on us for a long time. The welcome was very warm. The little church was built of mud.

The presence of the Lord was tangible. The praise and worship was out of this world. There were no musical instruments, the people were clapping their hands and singing from the depths of their hearts. It was awesome. Time came for me to give my testimony I said it as the Lord led me. In the middle of my testimony God began to move, people were getting healed, devils were leaving people, some were being filled with the Holy Spirit. I was unable to stand anymore. I just leaned on the wall. So filled was I with the Holy Spirit. This continued for some time. We just let God have His own way. The pastor invited us to return to the midweek service. We did so.

Afterwards we went to fellowship with the others in the large church. Our colleagues said that they could see joy manifest in our faces. We were eager to testify about what the Lord had done to that village. In the evening during the crusade the pastor brought all the people who were healed. Some of them had been bedridden for days. He said that most of the children were orphans and were suffering from HIV and AIDS related sicknesses. We advised him to take them to the doctors to prove that the HIV had gone.

He wrote us a letter a month later to say the children were healed – that no virus was found in their bodies. I see HIV and cancer as the leprosy of these days. Jesus can heal all! In the ministry that I attend I see people suffering from these ailments being healed by the power of Jesus all the time.

So this first mission really encouraged us to continue the work of God. I was so excited all day. I decided not to sleep in my hotel room that night. I went to sleep in Vivian's room. When both of us were in deep sleep, we both felt a large reptile crawl into the bed between us. We both jumped out of bed at the same time and we were wondering what it was. When we described to each other what had happened we both knew it was an attack from the devil. We prayed and counter-attacked the devil. Previously if anything like that happened, I would have continued to sleep. Vivian advised me to get up and pray. Now if anything untoward happens while I am sleeping I get up and pray or rebuke the evil forces in the name of Jesus. Somebody later told us that we had upset the spirits of that village by our visit. We were not intimidated, we were looking forward to going there the following Thursday.

When we returned the following Thursday there very many people had gathered for that meeting we met in a hut belonging to a villager. It was so hot in there that we decided to go outside under a tree. The people sat on the floor. Vivian said I should preach.

I did not know how to preach. Before the meeting I had been reading my Bible and one thing kept coming to my mind. I shared the word with those gathered among the crowd. Before I said much, the Holy Spirit began to move. The people were weeping, manifesting and all sorts of strange things were happening. When we left, a lot of them were still slain in the Spirit and were lying down on the floor.

During the crusade everybody kept telling me one thing. They said that I was going to meet my husband as soon as I arrived in London. I just laughed it off. One day we were praying in Vivian's room she saw a vision of me in a wedding dress. As she described the dress it matched the one I had three months earlier.

My Archbishop was preaching on remaining single and breaking that curse. He said that anyone who wanted to get married should go out and buy their wedding outfit. I did so by faith. Vivian continued to tell me that the man was not from our ministry but he was a very admirable person. I was so happy, and I thanked the Lord for it.

I kept dreaming that I was in a white stretch limousine, and a man was sitting beside me but I could not see his face. I saw my archbishop's wife coming to congratulate me on getting married. Many others came up to me and did the same thing. Sister Vania Kwawu came up to me and said that I was going to marry a man of God. I assumed that she meant a Pastor so I was remonstrating back her words. She kept speaking the same thing over and over again. I was very excited, but also somewhat apprehensive.

On my return from Kenya I was so exhausted from the flight and all that had happened in Kenya that I took a weekend off from going to church. The following weekend, my archbishop asked me to give my testimony of what had happened on the trip to Kisumu, Kenya. Apparently the man who became my husband was in the church promoting his first gospel music album. I did not notice him.

After the church service, my Brazilian friend and I were leaving for my home when we saw this young man walk towards us. He greeted us and gave us free CD's. I was pleased with the free CD. He spoke to us for a few minutes. My friend Marina immediately took a liking to him. On leaving the man came up to me and gave me a big hug. Now I was not happy with what he did as I do not like strange men getting so close to me. I felt offended by that hug. To add insult to injury, Marina kept saying how lovely and charming the young man was. Then she added, "Mabel, that man is going to be your husband." I got so cross at my friend that our friendship ended that very day. But Marina is very discerning. She fore knew certain things about me before I myself did. Nevertheless she held her peace.

The following Saturday I went to the service early as I was an usher in the church. When I arrived for the service I was singing lustily and I was very happy. I took my place as an usher. The man I had seen before came again and stood next to me. He asked me if I knew the meaning of the song that I was singing. He gave me such a vivid explanation that I was amazed at his knowledge of the Word of God. He began to speak in my life and on the very subject that I needed to sort out, and I needed to make that decision soon.

God answered my prayer that time. All through the service he stood with me and helped me with my duties. After the service he asked if I could meet up with him during the week. I said no. He gave me his phone number and I just threw it in the bin. I refused to give him my phone number. As far as I was concerned there was no way I was going to give him my phone number, let alone meet him.

Week in and week out I refused to give it to him or even look at his phone number. It always ended up in the bin. My good friend Gifty was on very good terms with Joshua so I could not escape him completely. All my friends liked him. I felt at ease when I was around him, but nevertheless I began to think that he was interested in my friend Gifty.

Joshua used to come to our church but I had never heard him sing or see him perform. The first time I saw Joshua on stage I was so blessed. He sings with the anointing of the Holy Spirit. After he had finished singing he was sweating and obviously was thirsty.

We have a special usher who is delegated to give water and handkerchiefs to special guests and ministers. I assumed the usher would do her job and offer Joshua the drink and a handkerchief. She did not do so. I was watching from where I normally stand and noticed that. I became very angry. I was livid and I went up to my best friend Gifty to complain about how the other usher had treated her friend by not giving him water. I personally went up to him and offered him my personal water and handkerchief.

Later I discovered that Joshua had prayed a special prayer that morning. He had prayed as the servant of Abraham had prayed when he was sent to find a wife for Isaac as in (Genesis24:12-14). "Then he prayed, O Lord God of my master Abraham, give me success today, and show kindness to my master Abraham. See I am standing beside this spring, and the daughters of the townspeople are coming out to draw water. May it be that when I say to a girl, Pease let down your jar that I may have a drink, and she says Drink and I will water your camels too-let her be the one you have chosen for your servant Isaac? By this I will know that you have shown kindness to my master."

Joshua had asked the Lord to do something special for him that day. So I no longer blame the usher for what he did nor am I annoyed at the way Joshua was treated. But the will of God had to be done!

Somehow I managed to give Joshua a lift in my car to go to his Hotel. My friend Gifty had insisted that I do that, because Joshua had no means of getting to his hotel. We chatted about various matters but I still would not give him my phone number.

One day he made me feel so guilty that I kept his number. I called him and we got talking and one thing led to the other. My archbishop and all the different pastors in the ministry blessed us.

We are now married. We live in peace, we minister together, and we choose to walk in agreement. Joshua is like my twin, my friend, lover, my pastor and husband. After giving up on all men and marriage and even vowing never to marry again I finally found my soul mate. Not only that. This is the first time I have done the right thing by the help of God. I call my marriage a miracle. I am not just married to any man but to an anointed servant of God, a good man, an honourable individual.

I want to encourage anybody who has been rejected, divorced, abused and broken hearted to come and meet with Jesus. He is the only one that can heal, deliver, save and restore. A good and peaceful marriage is not the only breakthrough that happened to me. My body is totally healed, my mind has been renewed and my finances have improved. I can say as in (3 John 2). "Dear friend I pray that you may enjoy good health and that all may go well with you, even as your soul is getting well."

Jesus has fought a good fight for me and I am eternally grateful. When I first got delivered my body felt so strange as if was not mine. I was not used to feeling like that. I was so light and free. I used to be afraid that the demons would return.

Getting to study the Word of God made me realise that I have the strong man Jesus. He is able to keep me. Also I have a responsibility to Him. I have to be accountable to Jesus. As long as I walk in his ways no harm shall befall me. I depend entirely on Jesus. I say all the time when all your hope is in Jesus there is no plan B. Jesus is the plan A and the only plan!

NOW I CAN BOAST IN THE LORD LIKE HANNAH IN (1 SAM 1:1-10).

MY HEART REJOICES IN THE LORD.

IN THE LORD MY HORN IS LIFTED UP.
MY MOUTH BOASTS OVER MY ENEMIES

FOR I DELIGHT IN YOUR DELIVERANCE.

THERE IS NO ONE HOLY LIKE THE LORD.
THERE IS NO ROCK BESIDES YOU.
THERE IS NO ROCK LIKE OUR GOD.

DON'T KEEP TALKING SO PROUDLY.
OR LET YOUR MOUTH SPEAK WITH SUCH ARROGANCE.

FOR THE LORD IS GOD WHO KNOWS
AND BY HIM DEEDS ARE WEIGHED

THE BOWS OF THE WARRIOR ARE BROKEN.

BUT THOSE WHO STUMBLED ARE ARMED
WITH STRENGTH

THOSE WHO WERE FULL HIRE THEMSELVES OUT FOR
FOOD.

BUT THOSE WHO WERE HUNGRY, HUNGER
NO MORE.

SHE WHO WAS BARREN HAS BORNE SEVEN CHILDREN.

BUT SHE WHO HAS HAD MANY SONS PINES AWAY.

THE LORD BRINGS YOU FROM DEATH AND MAKES YOU
ALIVE.

HE BRINGS DOWN TO THE GRAVE AND RAISES UP.

THE LORD SENDS POVERTY AND WEALTH
HE HUMBLES AND HE EXALTS.

HE RAISES THE POOR FROM THE DUST
AND THE NEEDY FROM THE ASH HEAP
HE SEATS THEM WITH PRINCES
AND HAS THEM INHERIT A THRONE OF HONOUR.

FOR THE FOUNDATION OF THE EARTH ARE THE LORD'S.

UPON THEM HE HAS SET THE WORLD.

HE WILL GUARD THE FEET OF HIS SAINTS.

BUT THE WICKED WILL BE SILENCED IN DARKNESS."

IT IS NOT BY STRENGTH THAT ONE PREVAILS.

THOSE WHO OPPOSE THE LORD WILL BE SHATTERED.

HE WILL THUNDER AGAINST THEM FROM HEAVEN.

THE LORD WILL JUDGE THE ENDS OF THE EARTH.

HE WILL GIVE STRENGTH TO HIS KING
AND EXALT THE HORN OF HIS ANOINTED.

REFERENCES

NEW INTERNATIONAL VERSION BIBLE

KING JAMES STUDY BIBLE

THE POWER OF POSITIVE PRAYER BIBLE

ARCHBISHOP GILBERT DEYA, "THE STRONGHOLD OF GENERATIONAL CURSES".

ARCHBISHOP GILBERT DEYA, "THE CURSES OF SEXUAL SINS".

Printed in the United Kingdom
by Lightning Source UK Ltd.
121590UK00003B/91-1800/A